Keys to the Kingdom:
Jesus & the Mystic Kabbalah

ABOUT THE AUTHOR

Migene González-Wippler (New York) is a cultural anthropologist and the author of over twenty books. She lectures frequently and has worked for the American Institute of Physics, the American Museum of Natural History, and the United Nations in Vienna.

TO WRITE TO THE AUTHOR

If you wish to contact the author or would like more information about this book, please write to the author in care of Llewellyn Worldwide and we will forward your request. Both the author and publisher appreciate hearing from you and learning of your enjoyment of this book and how it has helped you. Llewellyn Worldwide cannot guarantee that every letter written to the author can be answered, but all will be forwarded. Please write to:

Migene González-Wippler
℅ Llewellyn Worldwide
P.O. Box 64383, Dept. 0-7387-0593-4
St. Paul, MN 55164-0383, U.S.A.
Please enclose a self-addressed stamped envelope for reply,
or $1.00 to cover costs. If outside U.S.A., enclose
international postal reply coupon.

Many of Llewellyn's authors have websites with additional information and resources. For more information, please visit our website at:

HTTP://WWW.LLEWELLYN.COM

MIGENE GONZÁLEZ-WIPPLER

KEYS
—— TO THE ——
KINGDOM

Jesus & the Mystic Kabbalah

Llewellyn Publications
St. Paul, Minnesota

THIS BOOK IS DEDICATED TO MY STUDENTS

FIRST EDITION
First Printing, 2004

Book design and editing by Rebecca Zins
Christ illustration on page 114 by Wendy Froshay
Cover art © PhotoDisc, Inc. (Jesus image), © Digital Stock (wood texture)
Cover design by Ellen Dahl
Other illustrations by Llewellyn Art Department except for Figure 2

Library of Congress Cataloging-in-Publication Data
González-Wippler, Migene.
    Keys to the kingdom : Jesus and the mystic Kabbalah / Migene González-Wippler.
—1st ed.
      p. cm.
    Includes bibliographical references and index.
    ISBN 0-7387-0593-4
    1. Cabala and Christianity. 2. Jesus Christ—Messiahship. 3. Cabala—History.
I. Title.

BM525.G59 2004
248.2'2—dc22

2004048699

Llewellyn Publications
A Division of Llewellyn Worldwide, Ltd.
P.O. Box 64383, Dept. 0-7387-0593-4
St. Paul, MN 55164-0383, U.S.A.
www.llewellyn.com

Printed in the United States of America
on recycled paper

LIST OF FIGURES

LIST OF TABLES

INTRODUCTION

The word *Kabbalah* is derived from the Hebrew root *kibel*, "to receive." It refers to "receiving" secrets of the ancient Jewish mystics, who revealed them to their disciples mostly through oral teachings. Some of these teachings were encrypted in the Bible and other sacred books.

Kabbalah is best described as the esoteric doctrine of the Jews. It is mystical, paradoxical, and deeply disturbing. It is rather like a mathematical equation that cannot be solved. It is not easy to study and it is even harder to comprehend. Jewish tradition teaches that only married men past the age of forty can learn it—and then only after many years of arduous study.

Traditionally, women are forbidden to study Kabbalah. It is also taught by kabbalists that a thorough understanding of the Hebrew language is an intrinsic part of kabbalistic studies. This is true to some degree but it is possible to understand the basic tenets of Kabbalah without being proficient in Hebrew. Kabbalah speaks a universal language and it was intended for the entire world. This does not mean that Kabbalah will reveal its deepest secrets to everyone who is deemed worthy to study it. In fact, many learned Jewish kabbalists have spent their entire lives poring over the sacred kabbalistic texts, the Torah and the Talmud, without ever grasping its entire message. It is simply too vast and too profound. While no living being can ever hope to understand it fully, in the process of studying it, some of its precious secrets will be revealed to the earnest seeker.

Kabbalah does not unfold itself totally to anyone. It is like the many parts of a giant puzzle that are dispersed and divided among many but are never meant to be gathered and put together to form a comprehensive whole. As one goes deeper into its mysteries, it reveals some of its secrets . . . but not all. Each individual "receives" what he—or she—needs to understand.

In my first book on the subject, *A Kabbalah for the Modern World*, I explain how I, a woman and a Christian, first became interested in this abstruse subject. My answer to this question is twofold. First of all, a large part of my ancestry originated in Spain, which was the birthplace of many noted Jewish mystics and theologians, such as Maimonides, the famed author of *A Guide to the Perplexed*. It was also the birthplace of the first kabbalists, notably Moses de Leon, the reputed author of the most important of kabbalistic treatises, the Zohar, or Book of Splendor.

The Jews remained in Spain until 1492, when they were expelled from the country by Ferdinand and Isabella as a result of the Inquisition's horrors. They left behind a rich cultural and mystical heritage, which included the Kabbalah. These Jews were known as *Sephardim*, or Spanish Jews. Their name is derived from the Hebrew word *Sepharad*, "Spain." Interestingly, the word *Sephiroth*, which is the name given to the spheres of the kabbalistic Tree of Life, is derived from the same root. Therefore we can say that the Kabbalah has strong Spanish links and it is not surprising that many people with Spanish roots should be deeply attracted to it.

The other reason for my involvement with Kabbalah is that Jesus once said, "I am the Way. No one can reach the Father except through me." And, in truth, the entire Christian world is based on the scriptures and the Torah—the Law—as given in Jesus's teachings. These teachings are rooted in the Old Testament and therefore in the Jewish tradition. When I realized the importance of my Judeo-Christian background, I became determined to learn more about Jewish religious and mystical traditions. That is how I discovered the Kabbalah.

The Kabbalah is an esoteric theosophic system that contains Gnostic and Neoplatonic elements. It describes the nature of God and our relationship with him, providing an all-encompassing vision of creation. It also offers a powerful interpretation of the Torah and especially the Ten Commandments, which are presented symbolically as the ten Sephiroth or spheres of the Tree of Life.

Although the Kabbalah was not published in book form until the thirteenth century through the Zohar, its oral tradition is very ancient.

And it is clear through careful study that the entire body of Jesus's teachings are essentially kabbalistic. As I will show in this book, Jesus knew Kabbalah very well and sought to use it as a means of instruction.

Most importantly, the study of Kabbalah reveals a deeply messianic foundation. In other words, it is profoundly connected with the concept of the Messiah. This was made abundantly clear by the enlightened revelations of Isaac Luria, the Sage of Safed. The Lurianic explanations of the Kabbalah give a cosmic meaning to the Jewish suffering after their exile from Spain, and offer a messianic reinterpretation of the kabbalistic doctrine. According to Luria, the Messiah is at the heart of the Kabbalah, and only through him can its true meaning be revealed.

Luria's ideas paved the way for a major messianic upheaval centered around the figure of Sabbatai Zevi, which affected all Jews in the seventeenth century. Sabbatai Zevi had studied Kabbalah and the Talmud and was soon ordained a *hakam* (sage), a Sephardic rabbinical title. Unfortunately, he soon developed symptoms of manic depression characterized by strange behavior and violation of religious laws. During his manic periods he declared himself to be the Messiah and gained much support throughout Palestine and the diaspora. Later he was imprisoned by the Turks and converted to Islam to escape persecution. In spite of his disavowal of his Jewish roots, the Sabbatai Zevi messianic movement continued into the nineteenth century.

Although Sabbatai Zevi was eventually acknowledged as a false Messiah, the messianic foundations created by Luria's interpretation of the Kabbalah still stand. It is through the Messiah that the true meaning of the Kabbalah can be revealed, and through the Kabbalah, the true purpose of creation.

To Israel, the Messiah is yet to come. To millions of Christians around the world, he came two thousand years ago in the form of Jesus Christ. But Jesus was a Jew and so the concept of the Messiah is also Jewish. Only a Jew can be the Messiah, and to be accepted as the Messiah he must fulfill all the conditions surrounding this mystical figure.

In this book we will explore Jesus's claim to messiahship and attempt to determine whether he fulfills all the conditions required. According to Jewish tradition, the Messiah must be a male, directly descending from David through a patriarchal line. He should also be married and have at least one son. Many of Jesus's teachings will be reexamined in the light of the Kabbalah including the Paternoster, or Lord's Prayer, which is clearly based on the kabbalistic Tree of Life. A special method for praying the Paternoster will also be given, which will forever change this prayer for every Christian.

As we have seen, the Messiah is at the heart of the Kabbalah and only through him can its true meaning be revealed. In the light of this revelation, Jesus's claim to messiahship is very important because if Jesus was indeed the Messiah, then Christianity—his teachings—holds the keys to the true meaning of the Kabbalah and the purpose of creation. These are the keys to the kingdom, where the "kingdom" is the Earth. This does not mean that the Kabbalah is not Jewish. What it means is that Christians are Jews.

PART I

JESUS, THE MAN

CHRISTIANITY VS. JUDAISM

Now I am speaking to you Gentiles.
Inasmuch then as I am an apostle to the
Gentiles, I glorify my ministry in order
to make my own people jealous.

—PAUL, EPISTLE TO THE ROMANS 11:13

Christianity is a Jewish sect. It is based on the teachings of a Jew whose early followers were all Jewish. After the proclaimed death of Jesus on the cross, some of his disciples began to spread his teachings. The center of this indoctrination was Jerusalem until the year 70 CE, when the Romans destroyed the city. In those early times, all the converts into Christianity were Jews. Therefore the first Christians were Jews who believed in the teachings of Jesus.

When Paul wrote his Epistle to the Romans and spoke of glorifying his ministry "in order to make [his] own people jealous," the people he was talking about were his fellow Jews. Clearly, Paul's intention was to bring back into the folds of Christianity those Christian Jews who had left the movement. And he intended to do that by making them jealous of the Gentiles who had joined the new sect. He hoped that his fellow Jews would return to Christianity to reclaim their faith from the Gentiles. He did not succeed.

The primary source of the life and teachings of Jesus are found in the four gospels. Matthew is the first gospel to appear in the New Testament and the most influential in the church's history, but Mark is considered today to have been the first one written. The date given is sometime around 70 CE, just before Jerusalem's destruction. Matthew and Luke were written later. John, the last gospel, was probably written in the last decade of the first century, around 90 CE. Mark is believed to be the framework upon which the Matthew and Luke gospels were based. For that reason, these three are known as the synoptic gospels. The word *synoptic* is derived from the Greek and means "viewing at a glance." All three gospels present a similar view of the life and teachings of Jesus.

John's gospel, the last of the four, differs vastly from the synoptics, especially in the dates of events in Jesus's life. Also, in John, Jesus's ministry lasts more than two years. In the synoptics it only lasts one year. John is acknowledged as the "spiritual" gospel, dealing more with Jesus's divine nature and his relationship with God.

Of the gospel authors, only two—Matthew and John—were Jesus's apostles, but most biblical scholars do not believe they actually wrote the gospels that bear their names. It is now generally accepted that their names were used by their friends or disciples, though conservative scholars still believe that the fourth gospel, allegedly written by John the Evangelist, was actually written by him during his stay in Ephesus.

Matthew, an apostle of Jesus, was a tax collector in Capernaum, and it is believed his name was really Levi. Jesus is said to have changed his name to Matthew when he became an apostle.

John is said to have been the son of Zebedee and a brother of James the Greater, another apostle. John was very active in the organization of the early church and worked closely with Peter. He was later banished to Patmos and then went to Ephesus, where the fourth gospel is said to have been written. John is also believed to be the author of the book of Revelation.

Mark is believed to have been a Gentile. His Roman name was Marcus and his mother was Mary, a householder of Jerusalem, where early Christians held meetings in the times of the Roman persecution.

Luke was a close companion of Paul. He was also probably a Gentile because Paul distinguished him from his Jewish coworkers.

Other than the gospels, the New Testament gives further insights into Jesus's life and teachings through the Acts of the Apostles (written also by Luke) and the various Epistles.

After the destruction of Jerusalem in 70 CE, the Christian movement was dispersed throughout Palestine as well as abroad. An important source of the dichotomy or separation of Christianity from its Jewish roots was the increased number of Gentiles that began to join the new religion. By the end of the second century CE, Christian Gentiles began to outnumber Jewish Christians. Paul was largely the reason for the alienation. Convinced that he was the "chosen instrument" to bring Jesus's teachings to the world, he began to recruit large numbers of non-Jews into the Christian folds. To make Christianity more appealing he began to relax the traditional Jewish observances, which were difficult to accept by Gentiles, especially circumcision and the strict dietary laws. This was unacceptable to the synagogues and a subtle struggle began to erupt between the new Jewish sect and traditional Judaism. Rather than to appease the rabbis, Paul sought to alienate them further. The Sabbath day was changed from Saturday to Sunday, and the dietary laws were dropped altogether. Suddenly pork and shellfish, traditionally abominations in the Jewish Torah but a routine part of the Gentile diet, were allowed to be eaten. Furthermore, the all-important high holidays observed by traditional Judaism were also ignored. Fast days were transformed into feast days. What Jesus, an orthodox rabbi, would have said about that did not seem to matter to Paul; he had free reign, Jesus was not there to stop him.

Paul's radical and unorthodox views met with strong opposition from Peter, who was a devout Jew. But Paul's tactics were gaining large quantities of followers to young Christianity, and Peter was eventually forced into silence. Slowly but surely, the fledgling religion drew further apart from its Jewish roots and soon it became an individual force—new, strong, and independent.

The early followers of Jesus numbered around two hundred. Among them were the twelve disciples or apostles and the seventy-two that Jesus sent ahead of him to "places he intended to go." These followers of Jesus were all Jews. After the crucifixion, most of those who became Christians were also Jews. They formed two groups: those who were of Jewish ancestry, and those who were not traditional Jews but lived in Israel and adopted and practiced the Jewish faith, known as proselytes. Therefore, in those early beginnings, Christianity was a Jewish sect.

Paul was a Jew as well as a Roman citizen. At first, Paul was against the Christian movement. He decided to journey to Damascus and round up the followers of Jesus to have them arrested. On the road to Damascus, he became blind and had a vision in which Jesus appeared and asked him why he was persecuting him. After this, Paul became a believer in Jesus, was baptized, and regained his vision. With the same zeal that he had used to persecute the followers of Jesus, Paul began to preach that Jesus was the Messiah. But his aggressive personality and forceful ways alienated many people, not only Christians but non-Christians as well. Perhaps to learn to subdue these violent tendencies, Paul withdrew from the world and went to live in the desert for several years. Upon his return, he began to recruit as many people as possible into the Christian movement. Those years in the desert apparently had not softened his temperament, for he continued to upset those around him, especially the orthodox Jews. Paul did not care who joined Christianity, both Jews and Gentiles were acceptable to him. All that mattered to him was that large amounts of people would join the movement.

Before this time, all the followers of Jesus observed the Mosaic Law. Paul changed all that. The important thing was to believe in the divinity of Jesus, even if the believers did not follow the laws of Moses. People were baptized, accepted, and became Christians.

Paul's new rules were not accepted by many of the Christian Jews who followed the Mosaic Law and did not want to abandon the practice of Judaism. These people were led by Peter. This was the first division in the Jewish sect known as Christianity: Paul's followers, who accepted anyone into their ranks, and Peter's followers, who wanted to remain faithful to their intrinsic Jewish roots. As time went on, this separation grew until a total separation became inevitable. Eventually both Paul and Peter were prosecuted and killed by the Romans. Peter was crucified—upside down as he did not deem himself worthy to be crucified as Jesus—and Paul was beheaded.

Rome did not tolerate new religions but accepted the practice of established ones. It was therefore politic for the Christian sect to declare that they were Jews practicing a form of Judaism instead of admitting that they were creating a new religion. But this state of affairs changed suddenly when a group of Zealots decided to revolt against Rome. After this it was no longer safe to be associated with Judaism. But as members of a new religion, Christians were persecuted as well. Faced with the decision of being persecuted as Jews or as Christians, the new sect decided to fend on its own. It was at this time that the leaders of the Christian movement decided to preserve the teachings of Jesus, which previously had been transmitted orally. That is why, just before 60 CE, the gospels were written. Undoubtedly, not all of Jesus's teachings were written down. Like many of Moses' teachings, some of these were secret and remained so. Some remained oral teachings and this is where Jesus's kabbalistic knowledge became hidden. As we will see, some of these kabbalistic teachings were unknowingly revealed in what is known as the doxology of the Paternoster.

The new Christian sect, fiercely persecuted by the Romans, went underground. Today we find lasting remnants of those early days in the Roman catacombs where Christians used to conduct many of their meetings.

The persecution lasted for centuries until it was abolished by Emperor Constantine the Great in the fourth century.

Constantine was a solar henotheist and believed that the Roman Sun god, Sol, was the visible manifestation of the creative force behind the universe. In 310 CE, on the eve of a battle against his rival Maxentius, Constantine dreamed that Jesus appeared to him and told him to inscribe the first two letters of Jesus's name on the shields of his soldiers.

The next day, during the battle, he saw a cross appear in the middle of the sun with the words "under this sign you shall be victorious." Constantine went on to defeat Maxentius, and the Senate hailed him as the savior of the Roman people. From that day onward, he saw Jesus and the cross as the bringers of victory. The persecution of Christians came to an end, and in 313 CE Constantine signed the Edict of Milan, which mandated tolerance of the Christian religion throughout the Roman Empire. Under his protection the first Christian church was established. He went on to preside over the first ecumenical council at Nicae in 325, and he built churches in the Holy Land, where his mother—later canonized as Saint Helena—supposedly found the True Cross where Jesus was crucified. Constantine was baptized shortly before his death in 337 CE, finally becoming an acknowledged Christian.

With the Edict of Milan, Christians could practice their religion openly, but by then a great deal of animosity between Jews and Christians had developed. Increasing numbers of people were converting to Christianity. Even after his death, Paul's proselytizing efforts continued to be hugely successful. He and his followers had traveled widely, disseminating Jesus's teachings and converting many people, not only Jews, to Christianity. But because Christianity still was cloaked as a Jewish sect, these conversions began to be dangerous to Judaism.

Long before the Edict of Milan, the rabbis had grown increasingly concerned that their religion might eventually disappear through the increasing conversions to Christianity. In order to safeguard Judaism the rabbis made a momentous decision. They decreed that a person could only be called a Jew if he or she adhered to the Mosaic Law completely. This forced many of the Christian Jews to choose between Christianity, with its lapsed Mosaic rules, and traditional Judaism.

Christians were quick in their answer to this challenge. They denounced traditional Jews as failing to see the light and refusing to accept the New Covenant between man and God. In his early Epistles, Paul had pointed this out, while still leaving a door open for Jews to join the Christian fold. The Gospel of John and the book of Revelation also accused Jews of being blind to the truth of the Lord. The Christian leaders underlined their separation from traditional Judaism by flaunting the Mosaic Law. In this manner they sought to test their converts. If they really believed in Jesus and wanted to join the Christian community, they had to defy traditional Judaism in all its forms.

By the time of the Edict of Milan, the division between Judaism and Christianity was so complete that it could not be mended. They were two different religions and the differences between them would keep them apart forever.

What makes this separation all the more ironic is that Jesus and his early followers were staunch traditional Jews who, in all likelihood, would have been profoundly dismayed at the rift that tore apart the foundations of the Jewish law in the name of Jesus. In the Gospel of Matthew, Jesus says that he did not come to abolish the law or the prophets but to fulfill them. He goes on to say that whoever breaks the least of these commandments will be called least in the kingdom of heaven. He was not referring to the Ten Commandments but to the entire Torah, which is built on 613 statutes. Among these are the dietary rules and the Sabbath day, both broken by the early Christian fathers. Others, like the time of the Jubilee observed every fifty years, and the forgiveness of debts every seven years, continue to be part of the Judeo-Christian tradition and, indeed, of most modern societies.

Like Paul predicted in his Epistle to the Romans, he became the apostle to the Gentiles and now only Gentiles are part of the Jewish sect known as Christianity.

2

THE SON

He is despised and rejected by men, a man
of sorrows and acquainted with grief.
But he was wounded for our transgressions.
He was bruised by our iniquities.

—ISAIAH 53:3

Inevitably, any discourse on the life of Jesus—"the man of sorrows" prophesied in Isaiah 53—must start with the historical evidence surrounding his existence. There was a period during the nineteenth century when biblical scholars doubted that Jesus had existed at all. These doubts were caused by the theological nature of the biblical records and the apparent dissension of some of the available information in the gospels. Later on, historical sources of the time, such as the Alexandrian philosopher Philo, Pliny the Elder and his nephew Pliny the Younger, Eusebius and most notably the highly respected Jewish historian Flavius Josephus, provided the much-needed evidence required to attest for Jesus's factual existence.

Philo mentioned Jesus's death under Pilate while writing about the Roman governor's ignominious career in Judea (see Yonge, *Works of Philo*). Pliny the Elder, who recorded all kinds of natural and supernatural occurrences associated with famous figures and sects, mentioned some of the portents that Christians said accompanied Jesus's birth and death. In a letter to the Roman emperor Trajan, Pliny the Younger recounted some Christian accounts about Jesus and some of his miracles. But it was the evidence of Flavius Josephus, in his *Antiquities of the Jews* 18:3:3 and 20:9:1, which provided the strongest testimony for the existence of the historical Jesus. In *Antiquities* 20, Josephus writes an account of the Jewish high priest Ananus, who convened the Sanhedrin, the rabbinical court, to prosecute James, the brother of Jesus, "the one called the Christ," together with others of his group, for the crime of violating the law. Ananus did not succeed in this attempt and was eventually ousted by the king, who deprived him of the high priesthood. Through this account, Josephus, in a most natural and unbiased way, lets us know that a man called Jesus, known as the Christ, and his brother James indeed existed. We know through the gospel records that Jesus had a brother called James. Later on, Eusebius quoted Josephus and *Antiquities* 20, adding that Jesus had been slain by the Jews, although he was a most just man.

In *Antiquities* 18, better known as the *Testimonium Flavianus,* Josephus goes a little further. The passage concerning Jesus reads as follows:

> Now about this time there lived Jesus, a wise man, for he was a doer of wonderful works and a teacher of such men as receive the truth with pleasure. He won over many Jews and many of the Greeks. When Pilate, upon hearing him accused by men of the highest standing among us, had condemned him to be crucified, those who in the first place had come to love him did not forsake him. And the tribe of the Christians, so called after him, continues to this day.

The *Testimonium Flavianus* is highly controversial and some scholars argue that it is most likely a Christian fabrication laid at the respectable feet of the much-honored Josephus. They claim that as a practicing Jew, Josephus would have been outraged by the Christians' assertion that Jesus was of divine origin and would never have written such a passage. Others counter this statement by saying that as a serious historian Josephus had to record the historical truth, however unpalatable it may have been to him as a Jew. In spite of the controversy, most modern biblical scholars accept the *Testimonium* as valid.

From a purely logical point of view, the existence of the historical Jesus does not need the verification of historians of the period. It is an accepted fact that thousands of Christians were persecuted and killed by the Romans. This persecution began about thirty years after the crucifixion. At the time there were people still alive who had known Jesus personally. Is it logical that people would follow the teachings of a mythical, nonexistent person to the point of allowing themselves to be persecuted and killed, particularly when such a person was said to have lived barely thirty years earlier? Thirty years is a very short time. Even people under thirty today know the events that took place during the Vietnam War. It is a matter of historical record. And there are those who lived during those years who can attest to the war events.

The existence of the historical Jesus is no longer in question. Most scholars today agree that he lived during the times mentioned in the gospels, although not all concur with what the gospels tell us.

But who was this man called Jesus? How much can we deduce from the gospel record? In this book we will be concerned with Jesus the man and Jesus the teacher, as well as his claim to be the Messiah.

Jesus was born in Bethlehem, the city of David, but grew up and lived most of his life in Nazareth, the city of origin of his mother, Mary, and his father, Joseph, a carpenter by trade. "Jesus" is a Greek rendition of his Hebrew name Joshua, or in full *Yehoshuah,* which means "Yaweh is deliverance." Historical records place his birth between 8 and 4 BC and his death around 29 AD/CE. The month of birth is unclear. He was certainly not born on December 25, a date chosen by the early Christian fathers to coincide with the pagan festival of Yule. Some scholars believe the month of birth to be March but this is far from being fully accepted.

The gospels of Matthew and Luke tell us that he was conceived by Mary, a virgin, through the divine intervention of the Holy Spirit. We will go into that later on when we discuss the mysteries of the Shekinah, God's female aspect according to the Kabbalah. Mark and John make no mention of the virgin birth. Indeed, they both introduce Jesus as a grown man, shortly before he was baptized by John the Baptist.

The accounts of Matthew and Luke vary in many details. Only Matthew mentions the visit of the Three Wise Men with their gifts of gold, myrrh, and frankincense, and the flight to Egypt to escape the slaughter of the innocents by King Herod. Only Luke tells of Gabriel's Annunciation to Mary, from where the Hail Mary was born, and only Luke mentions the shepherds and the angels attending Jesus's birth in a manger and the events of his circumcision where two prophets foretold he was the long-awaited Messiah.

But Luke gives us an interesting glimpse into Joseph and Mary's deep religiosity. He tells us that after the birth of the child, they brought two doves to the high priest in the temple. The doves were to be sacrificed to ensure Mary's purification after her confinement. This reveals to us that Mary and Joseph were very devout Jews and careful observers of the Mosaic Law. Therefore Jesus grew up in a household of extremely religious parents who must have instilled in him a deep respect for their Jewish faith. This must have created in Jesus a great interest in religious matters. Again, it is Luke who attests for that fact with his story of Jesus being lost momentarily at the age of twelve. His frantic parents found him in the temple discoursing with the rabbis, who were astounded at his wisdom.

Something of the greatest importance happened to Jesus after his short sojourn in the temple. He simply vanished. He disappeared from the gospels for eighteen long years. The next time we find him in both Luke and Matthew (chapter 3 in both accounts), he is a grown man and about to be baptized by John the Baptist. There is absolutely no known record of Jesus's adult life before his meeting John, who was related to him, being the son of Elizabeth, Mary's kinswoman. We know that he was thirty years old because Luke tells us that was his age when he began his ministry, shortly after his baptism. There is something palpably wrong with this astonishing leap in time from Jesus's early childhood into full adulthood. The fact that the first two chapters in both Luke and Matthew deal with his birth in some detail, and then suddenly in chapter 3 he is already a man, leaves us with the feeling that there is much material missing from these gospels.

In order to help us elucidate this mystery, we must begin by reconstructing what probably happened to Jesus after the age of twelve. In traditional Judaism, when a boy reaches the age of thirteen he reaches the age of legal maturity and begins to participate in the religious life of the community as an adult. This occasion is marked with the ceremony known as the bar mitzvah, which means "son of the commandment." At this time the boy dons for the first time the phylacteries or *tefillin*, small, square, black boxes containing a parchment with scriptural passages. They are attached with black leather straps to the forehead and the left arm and are worn during weekly morning prayers. He is required to appear in synagogue to read from the Torah, or the Law, the first five books of the Old Testament believed to have been written by Moses. The occasion is celebrated with a feast where the boy is surrounded by family and friends. Several rabbis are always present.

The custom of making a bar mitzvah feast is very old. According to Midrash, which are interpretations of the Old Testament, the patriarch Abraham made a bar mitzvah for his son Isaac. In the book of Genesis we are told that Abraham made a great feast on the day Isaac was weaned. The Midrash interprets this as Isaac being "weaned" from his evil inclinations. According to the Midrash, at the age of thirteen a person begins to develop the maturity and intelligence to make proper decisions and thus attains the ability to overcome his "evil inclinations" if he so chooses. This implies that this first bar mitzvah took place when Isaac was thirteen years old.

Were bar mitzvahs observed during the time of Jesus? We do not know for sure. But we do know that in those early times people matured quickly. At the age of thirteen a boy was considered old enough to marry and create a family of his own. Traditionally, boys and girls did not choose their future mates. This was left to the parents, who arranged such marriages for their children with people of their acquaintance with children of the appropriate age and background.

Did Mary and Joseph arrange such a marriage for their son Jesus? In all likelihood they did. This was part of the Mosaic Law. We know through Luke that they were devout Jews who observed the law faithfully. The first commandment given by God to humankind appears in the book of Genesis when he said to his new creation, "Be fruitful and multiply." This is a very important *mitzvoh* or commandment, strictly observed by all orthodox Jews. Indeed, so stringent is the Jewish law on this respect that all orthodox rabbis must be married in order to fulfill their duties. And, according to the gospels, Jesus was a rabbi who taught and preached at the synagogue.

If Jesus was married, as indeed he must have been according to Jewish tradition, why do the gospels make no mention of this important fact? Or did they, in fact, mention it but the segment was later expunged by the church's early fathers? That would indeed explain the abrupt transition in the life of Jesus from one chapter to the next, when he becomes a thirty-year-old adult just after the age of twelve.

If Jesus was married, whom did he marry? Did he have any children? We can glean some interesting facts from the gospels, which offer some tantalizing possibilities, if not probabilities. These concern two of Jesus's apostles. Before he named the well-known twelve, Jesus chose four disciples. They were Peter and his brother Andrew and James and John, the sons of a fisherman called Zebedee and his wife Salome. This Salome was not the Salome of reprehensible memory who had John the Baptist beheaded. The gospels do not expand much on her.

There are some curious facts about John and James. John, who went on to write the fourth gospel, was, according to John himself, the "disciple whom Jesus loved." At the Last Supper, he reclined his head on his teacher's breast. In the Gospel of Mark (3:17), Jesus further distinguishes James and John by calling them the *Boanerges*, which is a Greek word that means "sons of thunder." Some scholars have concluded through exegesis that this term referred to the brothers' zeal, but the gospel itself does not tell us so. We are left to determine for ourselves what Jesus meant by calling James and John the Sons of Thunder. Thunder and lightning are traditionally associated with the Godhead. Did Jesus mean to imply that the brothers had a divine connection like himself?

But perhaps the most fascinating account about James and John is the one related in the Gospel of Matthew 20:20. Matthew calls it the Request of the Mother of James and John. The biblical narrative is quoted here in its entirety:

> Then the mother of the sons of Zebedee came to him with her two sons, and kneeling before him, she asked a favor of him. And he said to her, "What do you want?" She said to him: "Declare that these two sons of mine will sit, one at your right hand and one at your left, in your kingdom." But Jesus answered, "You do not know what you are asking. Are you able to drink the cup that I am about to drink?" They said to him: "We are able." He said to them, "You will indeed drink of my cup, but to sit at my right hand and at my left, this is not mine to grant, but it is for those for whom it has been prepared by my father.

Undoubtedly, this is a most unusual request to be made by the mother of any of Jesus's disciples, unless she felt that her sons had an inalienable right to such an extraordinary honor, such as a hereditary right. If James and John were Jesus' sons, then it would be perfectly understandable that their mother should feel such a request quite natural and fair.

If James and John were Jesus' sons that would explain why he called them "Sons of Thunder." It would also explain his marked preference for John, the "disciple that he loved," and John leaning on Jesus's breast during the Last Supper. Furthermore, at the time of the crucifixion, while Jesus was on the cross, he said to Mary, "Woman, here is your son," meaning John, who was standing next to her. Then he said to John, "Here is your mother." And from that hour, says the gospel (John 19:27), the disciple took her, Mary, into his own home. This last show of preference seems to indicate a very familiar bond between Mary and John. Among the women waiting with Mary at the foot of the cross was Salome, the mother of James and John. Both Mark and Matthew tell us this. Mark is the only one who names her as Salome. Further in

John, he tells us that before his death, Jesus was walking with Peter and John was following behind. Peter said to Jesus: "Lord, what about him?" And Jesus answered, "If it is my will that he remain until I come, what is that to you?" This caused Jesus's followers to think that John would not die, something that John denies in the gospel (John 21:22). But clearly Jesus wanted John to remain with him until the end.

The ages of James and John are very important if they are to be considered, albeit theoretically, as the sons of Jesus. John was clearly very young, perhaps fifteen or sixteen. We know this because he died in Ephesus in 101 CE. If he was fifteen at the time of the crucifixion, that would make him eighty-seven at the time of his death. James was older and that means he may have been sixteen or seventeen. If Jesus was married at the age of thirteen, James and John could conceivably be his young sons.

But what about Zebedee, whom the gospels name as the father of James and John? There is very little to learn from the gospels about this elusive fisherman. Could his name have been used to conceal Jesus's paternity? Zebedee comes from the Hebrew word *zebed*, which means a gift, a portion of something given to somebody else. Were John and James "given to somebody else," a nonexisting person known as Zebedee, to hide the fact that Jesus was their real father?

There are precious few conclusions to be drawn from the gospel evidence. We can only theorize. Jesus may or may not have been the father of James and John. But one thing is clear: the eighteen lost years of Jesus are no coincidence. Something was expurgated from the gospels, something that, left intact, would have revealed Jesus the man, his humanity, his true essence, and that which identified him not only as the Son of God but as the Son of Man.

3

THE FATHER

In the beginning when God created
the heaven and the earth,
the earth was a formless void and
darkness covered the face of the deep.

—GENESIS I

When Jesus spoke about the Father in the gospels he was refer-ring to the Almighty Creator of the book of Genesis. But, in-terestingly enough, Jesus did not describe God in the gospels. He spoke only about the Father and his relationship to his Father, and included his disciples as also sons of the Father, but did not expand on God's true essence—what or whom he really was. Most of the time when he refers to the divine being, which is rarely, he calls him the Lord your God (Matt 4:7, 10). That he elaborated further on the Creator and his powers to his disciples there can be no doubt, but these teachings were not revealed in the gospels. They were secret teachings and we can only garner some of their details through the kabbalistic prayer known as the Paternoster and some of his instructions to his disciples. We will discuss the prayer and other teachings in a later chapter.

The book of Genesis opens with the words, "In the beginning God created the heaven and the earth." But the Kabbalah has a shocking revelation about this creation. It tells us that the immanent, omnis-cient, omnipotent, and eternal cosmic force that we identify as God *did not* create the universe. Indeed, God, the ultimate being from which everything emanates, is *never* mentioned in the Bible.

The original Hebrew in which Genesis was written uses the following transliterated words to describe creation: "Berashith bera Elohim . . ."

The meaning of these words is, "In the beginning, God created . . ." The name of God used in this phrase is Elohim. But Elohim is *not* God. The true name of God is Ain Soph and this name never appears in the biblical scriptures.

What Kabbalah tells us is that the Ain Soph emanated Elohim so that this emanated force would create the universe. This secondhand creation by the Ain Soph took place because its energy is too vast and too powerful and needed to be "diluted" so that creation could take place.

Therefore, Elohim, the "God" mentioned in Genesis, is a creation of Ain Soph and is not really "God" in the cosmic sense of the word. Throughout the Bible, God is referred to in many ways. We read about God, the Lord, the Lord God, and other similar titles. In the original Hebrew we find specific names for the Godhead, such as Elohim, Eheieh, Adonai, and the Tetragrammaton or Yaweh. This last name, often and erroneously pronounced "Jehovah," is so sacred that devout Jews never utter it. It is known as the four-letter name of God—hence the Greek term *Tetragrammaton*, which means literally the "great name of four letters." In ancient times, it was only pronounced once a year by the high priest in the holy of holies in the temple.

Each name or title of the Godhead refers to a specific quality or series of qualities of the ultimate creative force.

Kabbalah gives us a very detailed description of creation. It tells us that before Ain Soph decided to manifest his essence through creation, there was only his all-pervasive light extending throughout the void. In fact, there is an even greater aspect of Ain Soph, known only as Ain, or the limitless, which precedes the light of Ain Soph. Ain is undifferentiated energy, pure thought, where there is No-Thing but sublime awareness. Ain expressed this awareness as the light of Ain Soph.

But Ain Soph knew that, being the All, he had to restrict his light in order to manifest his essence. He therefore created a vacuum within himself, and through that empty space projected a single ray of his light, which became known as the Ain Soph Aur. The ray of light traversed the vacuum in a series of ten concentric circles or spheres that were later to be called Sephiroth. The sum of the Sephiroth was the divine entity called Elohim. So we can say that the Sephiroth created the universe.

The ten Sephiroth are known collectively in the Kabbalah as the Tree of Life. But the light of the Ain Soph was still too strong to be manifested as a material world. Therefore the Ain Soph repeated this process four times. Each group of Sephiroth was weaker in strength than the one preceding it. In Kabbalah these are known as the four worlds.

The first world is known as Atziluth or the World of Emanation; the second is Briah, the World of Creation; the third is Yetzirah, the World of Formation; and the fourth is Assiah, the World of Action. This last world corresponds to the physical universe as we know it. The four worlds were emanated because the power of Ain Soph is so incomprehensibly immense that a vast distance must, by necessity, separate it from us. To retain our separate identities in the material world—Assiah—we must exist at an immeasurably great distance from Ain Soph or we would be annihilated.

Each of these four worlds is composed of a Tree of Life with its corresponding ten Sephiroth. We will discuss the Tree of Life in detail in another chapter.

Kabbalah goes on to say that there is a fifth world, and this world is the Ain Soph. There is a clue to the existence of these five worlds in Genesis, and this clue is the fact that the word "light" is mentioned five times before the first day is created. First "God"—Elohim—created light and there was light. Then God *saw* the light, divided the light from the darkness and finally he called the light "day." This process was followed by the rest of creation. But creation did not stop at that moment. Kabbalah teaches that creation is an ongoing process. The Ain Soph emanates his light continuously. Thus creation is renewed by God every billionth of a billionth of a second. If he were to withdraw his essence for one instant, everything—from the greatest galaxies to the tiniest subatomic particle—would cease to exist, and would revert back to the Ain Soph.

Physicists tell us that the universe is about 15 billion years old. Interestingly enough, seven hundred years ago a renowned kabbalist by the name of Isaac of Acco concluded that this was precisely the number of years that had transpired since creation. Isaac of Acco came to this conclusion through one of the verses in Psalm 90, which, according to an ancient tradition, was written by Moses. Verse 4 of this psalm says, "For a thousand years in thy sight are but as yesterday." From this verse, Rabbi Isaac deduced that a "God day" corresponds to one thousand man years. Genesis says that creation consisted of seven days. Kabbalah teaches that there were seven cycles of creation, each of which lasted seven thousand years. We are now living in the seventh cycle that began with the creation of Adam. The first six cycles before Adam were counted in God years. The seventh or Adam cycle is counted in man years because that is when humanity was first created. A "God year" equals 365,000 man years. Six cycles of seven thousand years each add up to 42,000. If we multiply 365,000 by 42,000 we come to the sum of 14,330,000,000 plus the age of the present seventh cycle, which, in 2003, according to the Jewish calendar, is 5764. The Jewish calendar counts time from the creation of Adam, which according to tradition happened 5764 years ago.

There is a great deal of concurring evidence between what physics and the Kabbalah tell us about creation. In my first book on the subject, *A Kabbalah for the Modern World*, I discuss in detail the parallels between science and Kabbalah.

So we have a fifteen-billion-year-old universe created by a force beyond human comprehension known as the Ain Soph through his emanation of Elohim. What happened afterwards?

When the Ain Soph created a vacuum or empty space in the midst of his all-pervading light, this empty space was dark and without form. This is the darkness that Genesis refers to and which "God"—Elohim—separated from the light. In Kabbalah, darkness is equated with evil. But evil is not "bad" in the kabbalistic concept. It is simply separation from God, from his light. Why should God create darkness or evil? To answer that question we must delve further into the act of creation itself.

As God's immense energy in the form of light traversed the darkness it made concentric circles, the Sephiroth. These Sephiroth are also known as vessels or containers. What they contained was the Ain Soph's light. But the power of this light was so immense that they broke under the strain. Some of the pieces or shards of these vessels flew away from them while others reunited to re-form the vessels. When the vessels were reunited, they became known as *partzufim*.

The word *partzufim* comes from the Greek word *partzuf*, meaning "persona." Partzufim is plural and it refers to the fact that the vessels or Sephiroth, upon reuniting, did so in five groups. The first three partzufim corresponded to the first three Sephiroth of the Tree of Life, each of which became a partzuf. The fourth partzuf was formed by the fourth to the ninth Sephiroth. The fifth partzuf was the tenth sphere or Sephiroth. All five partzufim are embodied in Elohim. Thus we can say that the Sephiroth, as Elohim, created the universe. It is interesting that Elohim is a plural word and that in the original Hebrew it is formed of five letters. In Kabbalah, these five letters represent the partzufim. But even though the ten Sephiroth broke and some of their pieces were re-formed as the partzufim, in Kabbalah they continue to exist and are still called Sephiroth. Kabbalists explain this incongruity by the fact that these events took place in a spiritual dimension where time does not exist. In this spiritual dimension, once something exists, it exists always. Therefore the spheres of the Tree of Life can exist simultaneously as both the Sephiroth and the partzufim in this other dimension.

The shards or pieces of the vessels fell at the bottom of the Tree of Life and became known as the Qlippoth. These shells or pieces formed another tree, an evil realm populated with dark forces.

An obvious question comes to mind on the breakage of the vessels. Why did the Ain Soph send so much force into these vessels? How could the Ain Soph, who is omniscient and omnipotent, not know that the vessels would break under such an immense strain? The answer is that he knew. But if he knew they would break, why did he send so much of his light into them?

Kabbalah teaches that the Ain Soph's main purpose in this awesome cosmic plan was the ultimate and quintessential part of creation: humanity. And the Ain Soph, in his great love for humanity, wanted to bestow upon it the greatest of divine gifts, that of free will. But in order to have free will, human beings had to be able to distinguish between good and evil, where evil is understood as the separation from God. Therefore the Ain Soph began by creating the darkness of the empty space or vacuum separating it from his light. Then as the ray of light known as the Ain Soph Aur traversed the darkness, he allowed the Sephiroth or vessels of light to break so that some of its pieces would fall apart and create the Qlippoth. This gave each human being the choice between good and evil. Each Sephiroth represented a divine quality in man, while the forces of the Qlippoth represented his negative tendencies. It was up to each individual to choose through free will between good—as the various Sephiroth of the Tree of Life—and evil, as the various spheres of the Qlippothic tree.

Kabbalists teach us that Genesis presents two creations. The first account of creation is given in chapter 1, while the second account follows in chapter 2. Chapter 1 gives us the blueprint of creation, as it formed in the mind of "God," Elohim, while chapter 2 carries out the vision of the Creator in the physical world. But more important still, in the first chapter, or blueprint of creation, God says "Let us create man in our own image." Genesis 1 goes on to say, "So God created man in his own image; in the image of God he created him; male and female he created them." Two things are immediately noticeable in this account. First, God speaks in plural. He says "Let US create man in OUR image." Then he proceeds to create a man and a woman. The Christian version of this part of Genesis is that God was with Jesus during creation. This is clearly not so because God created a man and a woman "in OUR image." This tells us two things: first, that God was not alone during this creation, and second, that God is both masculine and feminine. Jesus was obviously not the female principle that was part of the Creator in this account.

Kabbalah explains Genesis 1 in a dual manner. The Elohim—"God"—is a plural term. This refers to the Sephiroth that form the Elohim, and which are ten Sephiroth or five as the partzufim. That explains the "us" in Genesis 1. But also it refers to the feminine aspect of the Godhead, which is known in Kabbalah as the Shekinah. The Shekinah is also identified as the Holy Spirit.

In the Christian concept of the Holy Trinity, this mystery is said to be composed of the Father, the Son, and the Holy Spirit. Traditionally, the Christian churches have always alluded to the Holy Spirit as "he." But kabbalistically, the Holy Spirit is a female force, thus she would be the Mother in the Christian Trinity. This makes perfect sense because how can there be a father and a son without a mother? We will discuss the concept of the Shekinah and the Holy Spirit in the next chapter.

After creating man and woman in chapter 1 of Genesis, God gave them "every herb that yields seed" and "every tree whose fruit yields seed" as their food. Kabbalah teaches that this commandment was observed until Noah. Only after Noah did human beings begin to eat the flesh of animals.

It was also at this time, before the 613 statutes that form the Torah were given to Moses, that human beings observed the seven laws of Noah (see Genesis 9). These laws are:

1. Thou shalt not kill.

2. Thou shalt not steal.

3. Thou shalt not practice idolatry.

4. Thou shalt not engage in sexual crimes, especially incest.

5. Thou shalt not take God's name in vain.

6. Thou shalt not eat the flesh of a living animal.

7. Thou shalt establish a system of law where you live.

The sixth law of Noah is interpreted as meaning that human beings must not be cruel to animals, but in reality it forbids the eating of animal flesh. The seventh implies the establishment of a legal system, including judges and a form of government.

After the creation of man and woman in Genesis One, we find that the Elohim, now called the "Lord God," is still in a creative mood. In Genesis 2 there were no plants on Earth because there was no man to till the ground. So the Lord God formed man of the dust and breathed life into his nostrils. He then planted a garden east of Eden and placed the man there. Then the Lord God made every tree grow "that is pleasant to the sight and good for food." And among these trees he also planted the Tree of Life and the Tree of the Knowledge of Good and Evil. According to the Kabbalah, the Tree of Knowledge of Good and Evil is the Middle Column of the Tree of Life (see the schema for the Tree of Life in chapter 5). Therefore the two trees are one in reality.

After placing the man in the garden, the Lord God told him that he could eat of every tree except the Tree of the Knowledge of Good and Evil, otherwise he would die. He then created from the ground every beast of the field and every bird of the air and brought them to Adam to name them. Until this moment, Genesis has not named the man created by the Lord God. It is only when he asks him to name the animals that the man is identified as Adam.

Adam means "man" but Kabbalah teaches that there is a hidden mystery in this name. Adam is made of the word *Dam*, which in Hebrew means "blood," and the letter Aleph (א), which symbolizes the principle of life and death, the "spark" of creation. To the kabbalist the union between Aleph and Dam, which results in Adam, is a symbol of a blood pact that is to be established between man and the Godhead. That is why all the covenants between human beings and the Creator, exemplified by the rite of circumcision, are blood pacts. That is also why in the Old Testament all the first-born males were said to belong to God. Israelites were instructed to sacrifice to God all the first-born males of their cattle. The near sacrifice of Isaac to God later on in Genesis can be seen as part of this tradition, as Isaac was Abraham's first-born through his wife Sarah.

The naming of the animals by Adam and the name of Adam himself are of great kabbalistic importance. For it is only by knowing the name of something or someone that we can identify and conceptualize them. This is at the root of kabbalistic meditation. In order to meditate on something or someone, we must know their name and thus be able to identify them. This is of particular importance with the various names of God, for Kabbalah teaches that the name of something or someone *is* that individual or thing. Therefore God is identified with his name. In other words, according to Kabbalah, God and his name—or names—are one.

After Adam named all the animals, the Lord God caused him to fall asleep, took out one of his ribs, and from the rib created the first woman, Eve. Adam himself named her Eve "for she was the mother of all living."

As this point in the Genesis narration, the serpent is introduced and it is described as the most cunning of the beasts of the field that the Lord God had made. This implies that the serpent was a very special being. The Hebrew word for "serpent" is *nachash*, but it also means "enchanter" or "magician." According to kabbalistic teachings, the serpent was indeed magical. It was a very high spiritual entity, functioning on the level of Yetzirah, the World of Formation. The nachash or serpent was in the Garden of Eden to tempt Eve, by the Lord God's own instructions. The Lord God wanted to test Adam and Eve. As they had the gift of free will, they could choose to either obey or disobey their Creator. And the Creator wanted to know which would be their choice. That is why he sent the nachash to tempt Eve and, through Eve, Adam. But the nachash, in its zeal to carry out the Lord God's instructions, did more than just tempt Eve. It forced her to eat of the forbidden fruit because the argument it used was very compelling. It told Eve that if she ate from the tree she would be the same as the Lord God. Now, there was nothing more that Eve wanted than to become closer to the Creator. And being like him seemed to her the perfect way to accomplish this. Accordingly, she ate of the fruit and gave some of it to Adam as well. But Adam and Eve were not sup-posed to eat of the tree. That was not what the Lord God had told the nachash to do. All the nachash had to do was tempt Eve, not compel her to disobey with such an irresistible argument. That is the reason why the Creator punished the serpent. It was not that it did something it was not supposed to do, but that it did it too well. It went further than its instructions.

The Kabbalah's teaching about the angels' capacity to do evil hinges on this very same notion. Kabbalists say that angels have a very limited free will and no inclination to do evil. But sometimes, in their zealous-ness to do the Creator's will, they overextend themselves, like the nachash did. They do more than they were told to do. This is when an-gels fall. They do not fall because they hate the Godhead, but because they want to be closer to him, to be like him as Eve wanted to be. This explains also the fall of the angels as related in the book of Enoch (see Charlesworth, *Old Testament Pseudoepigrapha*).

Adam and Eve's punishment for their disobedience was to be ban-ished from Eden. The Lord God then made tunics of skin and dressed them. These tunics of skin were physical bodies, for before their sin Adam and Eve were wholly spiritual beings. Now they became mortal and were condemned to live as ordinary human beings.

It should be clear from the Genesis narrative that Adam was not the first man created. The first man came into being in chapter 1. The Lord God created Adam and Eve as special beings, as prototypes. Their divine mission was to serve as holy examples to the rest of the human race. But through an act of free will they lost their divine condition. That is why the Creator drove them out of Eden, "lest they eat of the Tree of Life and live forever."

We know that Adam and Eve were not the first created beings be-cause when they were sent to Earth it was already populated by many people. Genesis 4 tells us that after he killed his brother Abel and was marked by the Lord God on the forehead, Cain went to the land of Nod, where he "knew" his wife by whom he had a son called Enoch.

This son also married, as did his sons and his son's sons. Later Cain built a city that he named Enoch after his son. If Adam and Eve were the first human beings created by Elohim, where did Cain's wife come from? Where did the wives of his sons and grandsons come from? And how could Cain build a city if there were no people to inhabit it?

According to the Kabbalah, the creation of the first human beings by the Elohim in Genesis 1 took place during the sixth cycle before the seventh or Adam cycle. These first human beings were equivalent to primordial man who existed several million years before Adam. Through the evolutionary process, which the Kabbalah recognizes as part of creation, these first humans advanced and developed until the seventh or Adam cycle, which we can identify as the Bronze Age. That is when the Jewish calendar begins to tally the various genealogies of the patriarchs beginning with Adam. It is not that the Jews believe that the world began around six thousand years ago. It was Adam's creation by the Lord God that happened at that moment in human history.

From the preceding kabbalistic account, we can see that the Father that Jesus referred to, according to the gospels, was not God but the Elohim. But Jesus rarely used the term God or Elohim in the gospels. He preferred to call the "Father" the Lord your God. In Genesis 1 the Creator is referred to as God—that is, the Elohim. But in Genesis 2, after he rests on the seventh day, he is no longer God, but the Lord God. In Hebrew "the Lord God" is the Tetragrammaton, commonly— and mistakingly—known as Jehovah. It was therefore Jehovah, "the Lord God," who created Adam and Eve. He is the manifestation of Ain Soph in the seventh or Adam cycle. The fact that Jesus preferred to call the Father the Lord God, as in Genesis 2, tells us that he knew the difference between God—the Elohim—and the Lord God—Jehovah. As this is a kabbalistic teaching, we can deduce that Jesus was definitely acquainted with the Kabbalah and that to him it was Jehovah, and not the Elohim, who had created Adam and Eve, the forebears of humankind as we know it today. The Father of humanity and of Jesus is therefore the Lord God, the Tetragrammaton, Jehovah.

4

THE HOLY SPIRIT

The Holy Spirit will come upon you,
and the power of the Highest
will overshadow you; therefore also,
that Holy One who is to be born
will be called the Son of God.

—ARCHANGEL GABRIEL (LUKE 1:35)

As we saw in the preceding chapter, the word *Elohim* is plural. It is composed of the feminine singular ALH (pronounced "Eloh") and IM. Since IM is the termination of the masculine plural, added to a feminine noun it makes Elohim a female potency united to a male principle, and thus capable of producing an offspring. The "offspring," in this case, is the created universe. The Christian concept of the Holy Trinity relates to this kabbalistic teaching. The Father, Son, and the Holy Spirit are really the Father, the Son, and the Mother. In the Kabbalah, the Elohim are seen as the Father and the Mother manifesting simultaneously to produce the Son, which can be identified with creation, heaven, and earth.

According to Christian theology, the Holy Spirit is essentially masculine, but the Hebrew word used in the scriptures to denote spirit is *Ruach*, a feminine noun.

The feminine principle of the Deity is also known in the Kabbalah as the Shekinah, the Great Cosmic Mother in whose fertile womb the universe was conceived. As we saw earlier, the Infinite Light that is God unmanifested is known as the Ain (Negativity). Ain Soph (the Limitless) is the "container" of Ain's infinite light. The ray of light that emanates from Ain Soph is Ain Soph Aur (the Limitless Light). These three planes of unmanifestation of the Godhead are known as the Veils of Negative Existence.

The main characteristic of Ain is bestowal, giving. As Ain is unconfined and is the ALL, he does not receive, for he is Everything. He can only give. Therefore he restricted his own light in the vessel or container of Ain Soph. The Ain Soph is seen kabbalistically as a female principle, for she is able to receive and to contain. But she only desires to receive in order to give, to impart. In order to bestow the light for the purpose of creation, the Ain Soph restrained her will to receive the light of Ain, causing the entire light to depart from her. She then became a vacuum, an empty circle within the Infinite Light, which surrounded her evenly, also in the form of a circle. A thin ray of light, the Ain Soph Aur, extended from the Infinite Light of Ain, and traversed the empty circle formed by Ain Soph, creating the Sephiroth of the four worlds we discussed earlier. From the pinpoint of light that is the Ain Soph Aur was formed the archetypal man or world of archetypes known as Adam Kadmon, the Body of God. This is the fifth and highest world.

The Kabbalah has an interesting teaching concerning creation as related in the book of Genesis. The first chapter of Genesis in the original Hebrew begins with the word *Berashith*, which means "In the beginning." This word begins with the Hebrew letter Beth, which means "container." Kabbalah teaches that the letter Beth was chosen by God himself to begin the narrative in Genesis because it represents the Ain Soph, the perfect container through which the light of Ain was restricted.

Therefore we see that Ain is a male principle and Ain Soph, the container of his light, a female principle. The kabbalists call the two principles, Ain and Ain Soph, the light and its container, "He and His Name." Because the Ain Soph is the means through which the light of Ain is manifested, she is seen as the first vestiges of Deity and thus is perceived as God.

As God's divine essence is both feminine and masculine, so is the Elohim, the first palpable manifestation of the divine light, feminine and masculine. Therefore he/she created the universe according to his/her essence in perfect duality, positive and negative, masculine and feminine. From the proton (positive) and the electron (negative) that form the nucleus of the atom to the male and the female of every species, everything in the universe follows this dual pattern. The male is considered positive because he bestows his seed and the female is seen as negative or passive because she receives the seed, contains it in her womb, and gestates it.

Therefore, according to the kabbalistic concept of the universe, the cosmos has a dual quality; that is, it is composed of a positive (masculine) and a negative (feminine) principle, which are balanced by a third, which is the result of their union. This resulting, balancing essence is known as Methequela, the created universe. The union between the masculine and feminine principles that form the Godhead for the purpose of manifestation or creation can be seen as a parallel of the sexual act.

Thus the initial proton that existed at the beginning may be seen as a form of cosmic sperm that fertilized the initial electron and formed the cosmic egg from which, after a period of gestation of billions of years, the universe was "born."

The prodigious concept of a universe created as the result of a cosmic copulation on a divine plane need not stagger the imagination. All we have to do is observe the natural laws around us to realize how everything in the observable universe—from the birth of galaxies to the miracle of electricity, the duality of night and day, the pollination of flowers, and the impregnation of animals and human beings—is harmoniously based on a negative-positive principle. And if, as Genesis tells us, man was made in God's image, sexual union must be also an attribute of the Creator, albeit on a higher cosmic plane.

As we have seen, the Shekinah, also known as the Matrona, is the female aspect of the Godhead in the material plane. As the male aspect, the Deity manifests as the Tetragrammaton, or Jehovah. The name Elohim denotes the union of the female and female aspects of the Creator.

The mystery of the Shekinah is one of the most zealously guarded in the kabbalistic doctrine. Her essence is intensely sexual, and she is said to hover over the marital bed when a husband and wife are having sexual intercourse. She resides only in a house where a man is united to a woman, where the sex act may take place between man and wife. The Shekinah is the Divine Bride, the beloved of Jehovah, the Divine Bridegroom.

To the kabbalists, the sexual act is a most divine and sacred sacrament. Men and women who are not sexually active or unwilling to procreate are considered spiritually barren.

The concept of virginity as a blessed state is unthinkable to a kabbalist or to a devout Hebrew. The ancient Hebrews placed an extreme importance on marriage at an early age because they believed, as do the kabbalists, that the marital act brings man closer to God and that the pleasure that is felt by a man and a woman during their sexual embrace is shared by the Shekinah, who hovers over the marital couch.

The Shekinah is called alternately the Daughter of the King and the Divine Bride, but she is also the Sister and the Mother of humanity. She is the architect of the created universe, acting in virtue of the Word that God uttered to her at the time of creation. The Word or Verb was conceived and begotten into action by the Shekinah, just like a child is conceived and given birth by a woman. That is why she is always present when a child is conceived.

According to the Kabbalah, there are specific times when sexual intercourse should be undertaken for the exaltation and glory of God. For ordinary persons the conjugal relations should take place after midnight because tradition says it is then that God descends to Paradise and therefore at that time sanctification is plentiful. The "sons of the doctrine," that is, Orthodox Jews and kabbalists, should defer their marital relations until the night of the Sabbath, when the Deity is united with Israel.

When a child is conceived, the Heavenly King and his Shekinah provide the soul, while the man and the woman provide the body. There is therefore a dual union taking place at the time of conception: in the metaphysical plane, that of the male and the female aspects of the Deity, and in the phenomenal word, that of the man and the woman.

From the preceding we can see that the Shekinah is the Holy Spirit of the Christian Holy Trinity. In Matthew 11:32, Jesus speaks about the unforgivable sin: "Anyone who speaks a word against the Son of Man, it will be forgiven him; but whoever speaks against the Holy Spirit, it will not be forgiven him, either in this age or the age to come." The reason why any blasphemy or offense against the Holy Spirit will not be forgiven is because she is the Shekinah, the beloved of Jehovah. The Shekinah or Holy Spirit never gives offense; her sole purpose is to give of her essence. She is truly the principle of divine love and compassion. Therefore to sin against her is unforgivable in the sight of God.

When the archangel Gabriel appeared to Mary and told her that the Holy Spirit would come upon her and the power of the Highest would overshadow her, he was referring to the Shekinah, who is always present when a child is conceived. It was the Shekinah who was to come upon Mary and overshadow her. He was not referring to a "virgin" birth that would be unnatural and against the Elohim's principle. Therefore, in the light of the Kabbalah, the concept of Mary conceiving Jesus through the Holy Spirit did not mean that the Holy Spirit would cause her to conceive on her own. Mary would conceive Jesus through the grace of the Holy Spirit, *like all other women who conceive a child*, for, as we have seen, the Shekinah must always be present during conception.

The concept of Immaculate Conception seems to hinge on a mistranslation of the Hebrew word *na'arah*, which means "a young girl." The prophets of the Old Testament preached that a na'arah would conceive and give birth to the Messiah. But this word does not mean virgin; the Hebrew word for virgin is *betulah*, and it does not appear anywhere in the prophetic books of the Bible. Somehow the Septuagint or Greek translation of the Hebrew Bible, from where all other translations came, mistranslated the word "na'arah" as virgin. Thus early Christian thinkers felt compelled to believe that Jesus, as the Messiah, had been born of a virgin. That is how the myth of the Holy Spirit as the divine spark that caused Mary to conceive Jesus was born.

The only gospel that speaks of Jesus being conceived before Joseph and Mary "came together" is that of Matthew. Luke mentions Gabriel's Annunciation but goes no further. Mark and John introduce Jesus as an adult and skirt the virgin birth. Therefore it is only Matthew's gospel that presents the idea of the Immaculate Conception. It is easy to understand that the early Christian fathers, wishing to strengthen Jesus's claims as the Messiah, would decide to add Joseph's concerns about Mary's pregnancy to the gospel narrative, as well as the angel who appeared to Joseph in a dream to tell him that the child conceived by Mary was of the Holy Spirit. Furthermore, it is also in this gospel that the prophecy about a "virgin" (na'arah) conceiving a child that was to be called Emmanuel is cited. This is clearly the prophecy concerning the Messiah, which did not speak of a virgin but of a young girl giving birth to the deliverer.

The messianic tradition clearly states that the Messiah is the Son of Man, not the Son of God. Throughout the gospels Jesus refers to himself as the Son of Man. He never intimates that he is the *only* son of God, to whom he constantly refers to as the Father. On the contrary, he speaks of God not only as "my Father" but also as "your Father," clearly referring to the fact that God is the Father of all human beings, not only himself. Nowhere in the gospel does Jesus refer to himself openly as the Son of God. Neither does he speak of himself as God, a concept that would have probably shocked and dismayed him.

The messianic tradition also says that the Messiah will eventually die and that his son will continue his mission. This immediately implies that if Jesus was to be considered as the Messiah, he must have had at least one son. If John the Evangelist was indeed Jesus's son, that would most definitely fulfill the messianic prophecy, for John went on to continue Jesus's work, spreading his message and writing not only the fourth gospel but the book of Revelation.

Another important factor to be considered about the Messiah is that his lineage had to be traced through David and on to Abraham. This could only be done through the father, never through the mother. Interestingly enough, it is the same Matthew's gospel that traces Jesus's genealogy through Joseph to both David and Abraham. According to Matthew, all the generations from Abraham to David are fourteen generations; from David to the captivity in Babylon, fourteen generations; and from the captivity in Babylon until the Christ (the Messiah), fourteen generations (Matt. 1:17). But how could Jesus's genealogy be traced through Joseph if Joseph was not his father?

This glaring discrepancy between the "virgin birth" and Jesus's lineage has been glossed over by the Christian churches. Some attempt to trace Jesus's genealogy through his mother, something that could never be according to Jewish tradition. Others fall back on the idea that Joseph adopted Jesus and that accounted for the genealogy. But adopting a son does not mean that he has his adopted father's genes. A genealogy through adoption is completely unfounded.

We are therefore left with the facts that the Holy Spirit—the Shekinah—is present at every conception, that the conception of a child must take place through a physical union between a man and a woman, that the word *na'arah* used to describe the mother of the Messiah does not refer to a virgin, and that Jesus's genealogy is traced through Joseph. What all of this means is that Jesus was born through a natural union between Mary and Joseph, her husband, who was Jesus's biological father. There was no taint and no shame in this conception. It was natural, it was normal, and it was blessed by the Holy Spirit, as are all unions between a man and his wife.

Not only were the Christian fathers determined to testify that Jesus was born through a virgin birth, but they also insisted that both Joseph and Mary remained in this virginal state throughout their entire lives. Unfortunately for this further testimony of perennial virginity, all the gospels, from Matthew to John, mention the fact that Jesus had brothers, a fact that goes a long way to proving that Joseph and Mary led a normal husband and wife relationship. Mark mentions Jesus's brothers in chapter 3:31, Luke in chapter 8:19, and John in chapter 7:3. Even Matthew, who presented the concept of the Immaculate Conception, was not willing to perpetuate Mary's and Joseph's virginity. He also speaks of Jesus's brethren in chapter 12:46.

If Jesus was the Messiah, he had to fulfill all the messianic prophecies. He had to be born through a normal birth, he had to be married, and he had to have at least one son who would continue his mission. You cannot have Jesus be born through a virgin birth and be a life-long celibate and still claim he was the Messiah. You cannot have it both ways. Either he was the Messiah or he was not. If he was, then he had to be the Messiah according to the ancient Jewish tradition.

Jesus himself believed he was the Messiah. This message is found throughout all the gospels. In John 4:25, the Samaritan woman told him that she knew the Messiah was coming. Jesus said to her: "I who speak to you am He." If Jesus thought he was the Messiah, he would observe the messianic tradition that clearly said he had to be married and have a son.

Perhaps the most important of the messianic prophecies is that the Messiah would do nothing to change the Torah—the Mosaic Law. As we saw in chapter 2, after the crucifixion, Paul and his followers broke many of the statutes of the Torah. They tossed out the dietary laws, they changed the Sabbath day from Saturday to Sunday, they turned fast days into feast days, and generally thumbed up their noses at the rabbinical structure. These offenses, plus all the other anti-messianic details on the life of Jesus propounded by the early Christians, convinced the rabbis that Jesus could not have been the Messiah. But Jesus himself did not alter the Torah. In fact, as we have already seen, he said that he did not come to destroy the law but to fulfill it. He was an orthodox rabbi who taught in the synagogues. He would have been appalled by the actions of Paul and his followers. Therefore his claim that he was the Messiah must be given serious consideration. Many of the prophets of the Old Testament foresaw Jesus's coming as the Messiah. Among them were Isaiah 53:3,8; Micah 5:2; David's Psalm 22, and Daniel 9:26. Daniel went so far as to prophecy that the Messiah would be killed before the destruction of the second temple. The temple was destroyed by the Romans in 70 CE, about forty years after the crucifixion (see Josephus, *Works of Josephus*).

While Jesus was on the cross, he made reference to Psalm 22 to impress upon those of his followers who were present that he was the Messiah. What he did was cry out, "My God, my God, why have you forsaken me?" (Matt. 27:46). Many people who are unfamiliar with the scriptures believe that Jesus's faith weakened at that moment. Even those who are supposed to know their Bible sometimes misinterpret this saying of Jesus. Once, during a sermon at High Mass, I heard a Catholic Monsignor refer to this cry of Jesus as a proof of his humanity. Even Jesus, he said, had a moment of weakness on the cross.

But Jesus had no moment of weakness. He was quoting directly from Psalm 22, which begins with those exact words: My God, My God, why have you forsaken me? The relevance of this psalm to Jesus as the Messiah cannot be overemphasized. The one who wrote those words was David, the last Messiah before Jesus. And in the psalm David goes on to say, "They pierced My hands and My feet. They divide My garments among them and for My clothing they cast lots." All these things were done to Jesus during the crucifixion. In Psalm 22 David prophesied what would happen to him, the Messiah, in a future incarnation. This was the reason why Jesus cited the beginning of the psalm from the cross.

The Messiah is inextricably linked to the Kabbalah. In the next chapters we will discuss the symbolism of the cross in the Christian Kabbalah and Jesus as the heir to the messianic tradition.

PART II

KABBALAH

5

THE TREE OF LIFE

Then the Lord God said, "Behold,
the man has become like one of Us,
to know good and evil, and now,
lest he put out his hand and take
also of the tree of of life, and
eat and live forever . . ."
—GENESIS 3

The Tree of Life—Etz Hayim—is a model of the created universe. It is made of the divine energies of Ain Soph manifested in the physical world. Everything that exists in the cosmos, from the brightest galaxies to the tiniest grain of sand, is found in the Tree of Life. For this reason, the tree has been compared to a gigantic filing cabinet. In many ways the tree is the sum of all that exists. It is reality, it is awareness, it is the essence of being. Beyond the physical reality of the universe—the Tree of Life—is the infinite light of the three veils of unmanifested existence: Ain, Ain Soph, and Ain Soph Aur, which we commonly know as God. Like an artist who stands back from a finished masterpiece to view his work and perhaps add a few finishing touches, God observes the universe from without its boundaries and decides when and if to improve upon it. Like the artist, he can destroy his work or polish it further. This is done by God through the continuing outpouring of his light upon his creation.

The Tree of Life is the manifestation of God's creative impulse through the point of light that is the Ain Soph Aur. The entire gamut of physical existence is contained in that single atom of divine light. To

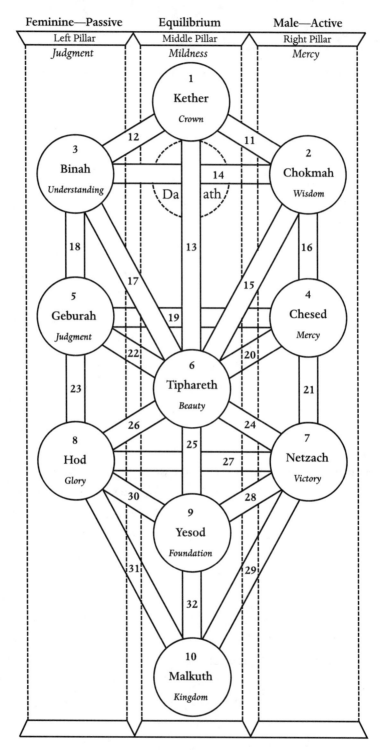

Figure 1: The Tree of Life and the Paths.

partake of the Tree of Life is to partake of God's infinite light. It is to be eternal, like the Creator. That is why the Lord God took Adam out of the Garden of Eden, "lest he eat of the Tree of Life and live forever."

The Tree of Life is made of ten Sephiroth or spheres, known individually as Sephira. These ten Sephiroth are divided into three columns (see Figure 1) and are also connected by lines known as "Paths." These Paths represent the twenty-two letters of the Hebrew alphabet, but the Kabbalah speaks of thirty-two Paths. The additional ten Paths are the Sephiroth themselves. Collectively, they are known as the Thirty-Two Paths of Wisdom.

While the ten Sephiroth represent different stages of manifestation of the infinite light and thus of evolution, the twenty-two Paths are seen as phases of subjective consciousness by means of which the soul becomes aware of cosmic manifestation.

We saw earlier that God is referred to by many names in the scriptures. Each name refers to a different aspect or power of the Deity. Each of the Sephiroth falls under the aegis of one of God's names, an angelic order, and an archangel. Each Sephira represents a different human endeavor and personality trait, a cosmic principle, and also is identified with a part of the human body (see Table 1). As the Tree of Life is seen as the Body of God—Adam Kadmon—so it is also identified with the human body. Adam Kadmon is seen as the macrocosmus, and man as the microcosmus (see Figure 2).

The Sephiroth are known as numerical emanations and are symbols of the abstract forms of numbers from one to ten. They are also known as the Ten Holy Emanations. The right-hand column of the Tree is known as the Pillar of Mercy to which is ascribed the male-active potency. The left-hand column is known as the Pillar of Judgment or Severity to which is ascribed the female-passive principle. The middle column, also known as the Pillar of Mildness or Equilibrium, is the harmonizing factor that blends and harmonizes the Right and the Left-Hand Pillars.

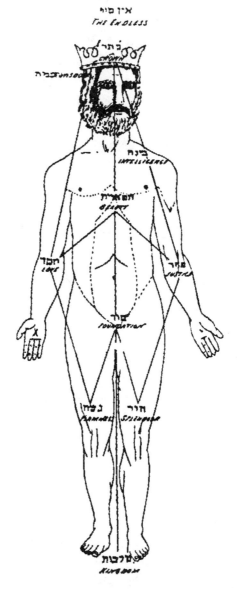

Figure 2: Adam Kadmon, the Body of God.
The various Sephiroth of the Tree of Life are marked on the figure.

GENERAL CORRESPONDENCES
OF THE TREE OF LIFE

Sephiroth	Planet	Physical Correspondences	Symbols	Image	Virtue	Vice
1. Kether	First Swirlings	Cranium	Point, swastika	Bearded king in profile	Attainment	——
2. Chokmah	Zodiac	Right side of face	Phallus, straight line	Bearded male	Devotion	——
3. Binah	Saturn	Left side of face	Cup, female sexual organs	Matron	Silence	Avarice
4. Chesed	Jupiter	Right arm	Orb, tetrahedron	Crowned and throned king	Obedience	Tyranny
5. Geburah	Mars	Left arm	Pentagon, sword	Warrior in his chariot	Courage	Destruction
6. Tiphareth	Sun	Breast	Cube	Majestic king, child, sacrificed king	Devotion to the Great Work	Pride
7. Netzach	Venus	Right loin, hip, leg	Rose, lamp, girdle	Lovely naked woman	Unselfishness	Lust
8. Hod	Mercury	Left loin, hip, leg	Names, versicles, apron	Hermaphrodite	Truthfulness	Dishonesty
9. Yesod	Moon	Reproductive organs	Perfumes, sandals	Beautiful naked man	Independence	Idleness
10. Malkuth	Earth	Feet, anus	Equal-armed cross	Young woman, crowned and throned	Discrimination	Inertia

Table 1.

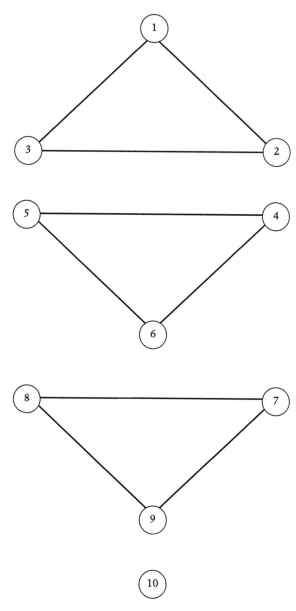

Figure 3: The Triads of the Tree of Life.

Each Sephira is androgynous or "bisexual" in essence because it is feminine or receptive to the Sephira that precedes it and masculine or transmissive to the Sephira that follows it.

The Middle Pillar controls the outpouring of the positive or negative energies that emanate from the Sephiroth of the Right or the Left-Hand Pillars. The Right-Hand Pillar or Pillar of Mercy has the quality of "limitless bestowal," while the Left-Hand Pillar or Pillar of Judgment has the quality of "limitless restraint." If a human being, by virtue of a good action, deserves the bestowal of positive energy from the Pillar of Mercy, this pillar would bestow of its essence endlessly. On the other hand, the Pillar of Judgment would restrain this flow and the person would not receive the rightful amount of positive energy that was deserved for the good deed. The Middle Pillar balances these energies equally.

The Pillar of Mildness acts as a mediator to control both the Right and the Left-Hand Pillar to ensure that the appropriate measure of mercy is allotted.

The ten Sephiroth are divided among the three pillars as follows. Sephiroth 1, 6, 9, and 10 are placed on the Middle Pillar. Sephiroth 2, 4, and 7 are on the Right-Hand Pillar. Sephiroth 3, 5, and 8 are on the Left-Hand Pillar. The Sephiroth also form three "triads" or triangles (see Figure 3). The first triad is formed by Sephiroth 1, 2, and 3, also known as the Supernals; the second by Sephiroth 4, 5, and 6; and the third by Sephiroth 7, 8, and 9. The tenth Sephira stands by itself. As you can see from figure 3, the first triad points upward while the other two point downward. This means that the first three Sephiroth or Supernals belong to a higher spiritual dimension than the other seven, and are out of reach from the ordinary human being. The number seven in the kabbalistic view of the universe is connected with the seven days of creation, the seven days of the week, and the seven planets of the ancients.

The ten Sephiroth were emanated from the Ain Soph in the following order (see Table 2):

THE COLOR SCALES
OF THE TREE OF LIFE
IN THE FOUR WORLDS

SEPHIRA	Atziluth King Scale	Briah Queen Scale	Yetzirah Emperor Scale	Assiah Empress Scale
1. Kether	Brilliance	White brilliance	White brilliance	White, flecked gold
2. Chokmah	Light blue	Grey	Iridescent grey	White, flecked with red, blue, yellow
3. Binah	Crimson	Black	Dark brown	Grey, flecked with pink
4. Chesed	Violet	Blue	Purple	Azure, flecked with yellow
5. Geburah	Orange	Red	Scarlet	Red, flecked with black
6. Tiphareth	Rose pink	Yellow	Salmon pink	Amber
7. Netzach	Amber	Emerald green	Yellow green	Olive, flecked with gold
8. Hod	Violet	Orange	Brick red	Yellowish black, flecked with white
9. Yesod	Indigo	Violet	Dark purple	Citrine, flecked with azure
10. Malkuth	Yellow	Citrine, olive, russet, black	Citrine, olive, russet, black, flecked with gold	Black, rayed with yellow

Table 2.

I. KETHER—CROWN

This first Sephira is the source of the other nine. It is ascribed number one, which encompasses within itself the other eight numbers of the decimal scale. It is undivisible but definable. And since definition projects an image or duplicate of the object defined, we find that by reflection of itself, number one projects all the other numbers. Therefore it is called the "father of numbers" and is a fitting image of the Father of all things.

Among the various titles given to Kether are Concealed of the Concealed, the Vast Countenance, the Primordial Point, the Point within a Circle, Macroprosopos, and Ancient of Ancients. The divine name ascribed to this sphere is Eheieh (AHIH), which means I Am That I Am and was the name given to Moses from the Burning Bush. Its archangel is Metatron, known as the Prince of Countenance and the Chancellor of Heaven. It is Metatron who brings other beings before the face of God. In some traditions, the angelic order is *Chaioth ha Qadesh* or Holy Living Creatures, while in others it is the order of Seraphim.

The color associated with Kether is white brilliance, and it comes from the Briatic color scale ascribed to the World of Briah, also known as the World of Creation. Each of the four worlds has its own scale of colors (see Table 2).

Kether's physical correspondence is the top of the head. The telesmatic image—a visual concept of a cosmic or spiritual force—associated with Kether is that of an ancient bearded king seen in profile. A "crown" is a kingly attribute that is placed on top of the head of the monarch. This Sephira is also known as the Head Which Is Not. In all this symbolism we see distinct correspondences with the human head, which, in the world of archetypal ideas, represents the highest level of consciousness. The Head Which Is Not is a clear image of a superconsciousness that lies outside the realm of human experience and thus cannot be encompassed within the limits of the human brain. It is the crown, the wisdom, that adorns the brow of the bearded king, who is none other than Adam Kadmon, the first manifestation of the Divine Light.

TREE OF LIFE AND
ITS HOLY CORRESPONDENCES

Sephira	Title	God Name	Archangel	Angelic Choir
1. Kether	Crown	Eheieh	Metatron	Chaioth ha Qadesh
2. Chokmah	Wisdom	Jehovah	Ratziel	Auphanim
3. Binah	Understanding	Jehovah Elohim	Tzaphkiel	Aralim
4. Chesed	Mercy	El	Tzadkiel	Chasmalim
5. Geburah	Severity	Elohim Gebor	Kamael	Seraphim
6. Tiphareth	Beauty	Jehovah elo ve Daath	Raphael	Malachim
7. Netzach	Victory	Jehovah Tzabaoth	Haniel	Elohim
8. Hod	Glory	Elohim Tzabaoth	Michael	Beni Elohim
9. Yesod	Foundation	Shaddai El Chai	Gabriel	Cherubim
10. Malkuth	Kingdom	Adonai Ha Aretz	Sandalphon	Ishim

Table 3.

Kether's sphere of operation, its first manifestation, is known as Rashith ha-Gilgalim, the Primum Mobile or First Mover, which bestows life unto all things in the universe.

Kether is outside human experience. Its essence cannot be comprehended by the human mind. In this Sephira there is no form, only pure being, because there is no differentiation into a pair of opposites yet.

In order to obtain an adequate concept of this formless state of latent existence, we may visualize it as a void, as interstellar space, which nevertheless harbors within it all the potential of life.

Another title given to Kether is the First Swirlings, which implies the activity of the cosmic energy at the time of creation. From these "first swirlings" sprang the second Sephira, Chokmah, the first to be differentiated in one of the two modes of existence, male and female.

2. CHOKMAH—WISDOM

This is a masculine-active sphere to which is ascribed the number two. It is also known as Aba, the Father, to whom the Mother—Binah, the third Sephira—is united.

Among the titles given to Chokmah are the Supernal Father, Power of Yetzirah, and Yod of Tetragrammaton. The God name is Jehovah, the divine ideal wisdom. The archangel is Raziel, the Prince of Hidden Knowledge, and the order of angels is Auphanim, or Wheels, also known as the order of Cherubim.

The color ascribed to Chokmah is a pearly grey. The telesmatic image is a bearded male figure. Its sphere of operation is Masloth, the starry heaven, wherein it determines the forms of all things. Its physical correspondence is the right side of the face.

If we can compare Kether to a point, we can compare Chokmah to a line, which is an extension of a point in space. This straight line or "uplifted rod of power" may be equalized with the phallus, which is one of the symbols of this Sephira.

Chokmah is essentially dynamic, for within it is the seed of all creation. Its quality is wisdom, which implies perfect knowledge and understanding. It is significant that the quality assigned to the third Sephira (Binah) is understanding.

3. BINAH—UNDERSTANDING

This Sephira is a female-passive potency, known both as Ama—the dark sterile mother—and Aima—the bright fertile mother, who is eternally conjoined with Aba, the father (Chokmah), for the maintenance of the order of the universe. Binah is the Supernal Mother, the feminine aspect of God as the Elohim. She is seen as Mother of All Living, the archetypal womb through which all life comes into manifestation. Binah is also known as Khorsia (the Throne) and Marah (the Great Sea), which is a root for Mary, the Blessed Mother of Christianity.

The number ascribed to Binah is three. The divine name is Jehovah Elohim, the perfection of creation and the life of the world to come. The archangel is Tzaphkiel, the Prince of the Spiritual Strife against Evil. The order of angels is Aralim, the Strong and Mighty Ones, also known as the order of Thrones.

The color ascribed to Binah is black, described as a thick darkness that veils the Divine Glory in which all colors are hidden. Its sphere of operation is Shabbathai, or rest, wherein it gives form to the forces of Chaos.

Binah is associated with the planet Saturn. Its telesmatic image is that of a matron or mature woman. Its physical correspondence is the left side of the face.

Whereas Chokmah is dynamic force, Binah is form, which is the container of force. The first letter of Binah is the Hebrew letter Beth, which, as we have seen, is the symbol of all containers.

In Binah and Chokmah we have the first two polarizing aspects of manifestation, the supernal Father and Mother, from which the universe sprang. Together, they are the Elohim, the Creator Genesis speaks about. They are the two primordial blocks of life, proton and electron, which constitute all aspects of creation. In this first pair of Sephiroth lies the key to sex, for they represent the biological opposites. They occur not only in space but also in time. We see them in the alternating periods in our lives, in the tides of the sea, in our physiological processes and international affairs. The alternating cycles of activity and passivity, construction and destruction are the interplay of these eternal opposites. It is interesting to note in this context that one of the symbols of Binah is the planet Saturn, also identified as Kronos or Time.

While wisdom is the quality of Chokmah, understanding is that of Binah. Wisdom suggests complete and infinite knowledge, while understanding conveys the impression of the ability to grasp the concepts of wisdom. The Father knows all, but the Mother understands everything.

Kether, Chokmah, and Binah form the first triad of the Tree of Life.

4. CHESED—MERCY

Chesed is a masculine-active potency emanated from Binah as a result of her union with Chokmah. Chesed is also known as Majesty and *Gedulah*, which means "greatness" or "magnificence." Its quality is mercy or love on a higher cosmic level.

The number ascribed to Chesed is four. The divine name is El, the Strong and Mighty God, ruling in glory, magnificence, and grace. The archangel is Tzadkiel, the Prince of Mercy and Beneficence, and the order of angels is Chasmalim, the Brilliant Ones, also known as the order of Dominions or Dominations.

Chesed's color is bright blue. Its sphere of operations is Tzedek, wherein it forms the images of material things, bestowing peace, love, and mercy. It is associated with the planet Jupiter. Its telesmatic image is that of a mighty crowned and throned king. Its physical correspondence is the right arm.

Chesed is the first Sephira that may be conceived by the human mind, for it is the conception of the abstract concepts formulated by the three Supernals, Kether, Chokmah, and Binah.

Whereas Chokmah may be likened to the All-Knowing Father, the All-Begetter, Chesed is seen as the Loving Father, protecting, forgiving, and generous. As Chesed lies directly under Chokmah on the Right-Hand Pillar, we can see that it reflects the paternal qualities of Chokmah on a lower physical level.

Between the three Supernals and the other seven Sephiroth lies a chasm known in Kabbalah as the Abyss. This pit is the demarcation of varying degrees of consciousness. The three Supernals represent those higher states of consciousness that transcend human awareness. The lower Sephiroth function within the realm of ideas and as such are the only ones we can grasp with our normal consciousness. In order to comprehend that abstract essence of the higher Sephiroth, we have to cross the gulf of the Abyss, which implies having to transcend the confinement of our conscious personalities to reach our Higher Self, the great unconscious.

5. GEBURAH—STRENGTH, SEVERITY

This Sephira is a feminine-passive potency emanated from Chesed. The titles given to this sphere are Din (Justice) and Pachad (Fear).

Geburah is ascribed the number five. The divine name is Elohim Gebor, the Mighty and Terrible God, who punishes evil and rules in wrath and terror. The archangel is Khamael, the Prince of Strength and Courage, and the angelic order is the Seraphim or Fiery Serpents, also known as the order of Powers.

Geburah's color is red and the sphere of operation is Madim, wherein it brings strength, war, justice, and vengeance. Its telesmatic image is a mighty warrior in his carriage. Its physical correspondence is the left arm. Geburah is associated with the planet Mars.

Geburah is the most forceful and disciplined of the Sephiroth. Its force is not evil unless its essence overflows from justice into cruelty. This is the symbolism of Mars, the Roman god of war and strife. To kabbalists Geburah is essentially a conciliatory force, a restriction of the merciful love of Chesed. Without Geburah's strong arm the mercies of Chesed would degenerate into folly, weakness, and cowardice. For that reason, Chesed and Geburah must always function together to ensure that justice is always tempered by mercy.

Geburah may be likened to fire, which may be used constructively or destructively. Its power for destruction may be curtailed by the careful control of the flame. In Geburah we also find the element of awe, the "fear of God," which, according to the scriptures, is necessary for salvation.

6. TIPHARETH—BEAUTY

This Sephira is an emanation of the energies of Kether and is located in the Pillar of Equilibrium or Middle Pillar directly under the first Sephira. Its titles are Zoar Anpin (the Lesser Countenance), Melekh (the King), Adam, the Son, and the Man.

Tiphareth is ascribed the number six and its color is yellow. The divine name is Jehovah Elo Ve Daath, a God of Knowledge and Wisdom ruling over the universe in love and peace. The archangel is Raphael, the Prince of Brightness, Beauty, and Life. The order of angels is the Malachim, the Angelic Kings, also known as the order of Virtues.

Tiphareth's sphere of operation is Shemesh, the solar light, wherein it bestows life, health, light, and brilliancy. Its telesmatic images are a child, a majestic king, and a sacrificed god. Its physical correspondence is the breast. This Sephira is associated with the Sun and with Jesus Christ.

In Tiphareth we see that by the union of Chesed and Geburah (Mercy and Justice), we obtain Beauty or Clemency, which completes the second triad of the Tree of Life.

Tiphareth is the center of equilibrium of the tree. As such it is a link, a point of transition. Kether, the first Sephira, is the divine spark in which exists the seed of manifestation. The next four Sephiroth—Chokmah, Binah, Chesed, and Geburah—represent the Higher Self. Tiphareth is the point of connection between these Sephiroth or Higher Self and the four lower Sephiroth which represent the Lower Self or conscious personality.

Two of the symbols ascribed to Tiphareth are a child and a sacrificed god. In the child we see a beginning that ends in the sacrificed god for the purpose of transformation of the material into the divine. This aspect of Tiphareth is the point of transmutation between the planes of force and the planes of form.

7. NETZACH—VICTORY

Netzach is a male-active potency, emanated from Tiphareth and Chesed. Its title is Firmness.

The number ascribed to Netzach is seven. The divine name is Jehovah Tzabaoth, a God of Hosts and Armies, who rules in triumph and harmony. The archangel is Anael, the Prince of Love and Harmony. The order of angels is the Elohim or Gods, also known as the order of Principalities.

Netzach's color is green, a combination of the yellow and blue rays of Chesed and Tiphareth. Its sphere of operation is Nogah, the External

Splendor, wherein it bestows love, harmony, and zeal. It is associated with the planet Venus. Its telesmatic image is a beautiful naked woman. Its physical correspondence is the left leg and hip.

Netzach represents the instincts and the emotions. It is a sphere densely populated with the thoughtforms of the group mind. Thus it is essentially an illusory plane, where the archetypal ideas have not yet been expressed as forms.

The planet Venus, which is ascribed to Netzach, is also a symbol of the Roman goddess of love. Venus is not a fertility goddess like Ceres or Persephone. She is pure emotion. And the essence of this emotion is never crystallized into form. Netzach, then, represents the instinctive, emotional side of our nature.

8. HOD—GLORY

This Sephira is a male-active potency and it is emanated from Tiphareth and Geburah.

Hod's number is eight. The divine name is Elohim Tzabaoth, a God of Hosts, of praise and glory, who rules the universe in mercy and agreement, wisdom and harmony. The archangel is Michael, a Prince of the Presence, of splendor and wisdom. The order of angels is the Beni Elohim, the Sons of the Gods, also known as the order of Archangels.

Hod's color is orange, a combination of the red and yellow rays of Geburah and Tiphareth. Its sphere of operation is Kobab, the stellar light, wherein it bestows scientific knowledge, clarity of speech, excellence in communications, and proficiency in the arts.

Hod is associated with the planet Mercury. Its telesmatic image is a hermaphrodite. Its physical correspondence is the right leg and hip.

Hod is the seat of the intellectual powers in human beings. It is the sphere where the emotions and instincts of Netzach finally take form and come into action. Like Chesed and Geburah, Hod and Netzach must always function together, for just as the instinct or emotion cannot be manifested without the creative power of the intellect, the intellect cannot manifest itself without the thoughtforms that arise out of instinct and emotion.

In the practical Kabbalah, Hod is the sphere of magic because it is the Sephira where forms are created. The practicing kabbalist uses this Sephira to formulate with his mind the images of things he wants to attain in the material world. Since Hod is the seat of the intellect or human mind, any thoughts projected from Netzach into this sphere may be impressed upon the higher consciousness, which will then bring the images thus formed into realization.

9. YESOD—FOUNDATION

This Sephira is located on the Middle Pillar, directly under Tiphareth. It is emanated from the union between Chesed and Geburah. With Netzach and Hod it forms the third and last triad.

Yesod's number is nine. The divine name is Shaddai El Chai, the Almighty Living God. The archangel is Gabriel, Prince of Change and Sustenance. The order of angels is the Cherubim, also known simply as the Angels.

The color ascribed to Yesod is violet, a combination of the red and blue rays of Geburah and Chesed. Its sphere of operation is Levanah, the Lunar Beam, wherein it bestows fertility, astral visions, and increase and decrease in human affairs.

Yesod is associated with the Moon. Its telesmatic image is a beautiful naked man, very strong. Its physical correspondences are the reproductive organs.

Yesod is the seat of intuition in human beings. It is the sphere of the astral light and the receptacle of the emanations of the other Sephiroth. The purpose of Yesod is to purify and correct these emanations. As the sphere of the Moon, Yesod reflects the light of Tiphareth's Sun. For that reason Yesod's light is always in a state of flux and reflux because the amount of sunlight it receives waxes and wanes in a twenty-eight-day cycle.

Since Yesod is the sphere of the Moon, it is ruled by all the Moon goddesses, such as Diana, the virgin Moon goddess of the Romans, and Isis, the fertile Moon goddess of the Egyptians. The reason why the Moon is sometimes seen as a virgin and other times as a fertile mother may be found in its cyclical rhythms and the estrous cycle of the female of every species.

The lunar rhythms coincide with the monthly cycles of a woman which regulate when she may be impregnated (fertile goddess) and when she may not (virgin goddess).

To Yesod is also assigned the water element because the lunar tides also affect the oceans and the body fluids in all living creatures. This magnetic influence of the Moon can only operate through the sphere of Yesod. Netzach, Hod, and Yesod form the third and last triad of the tree.

10. MALKUTH—KINGDOM

This last Sephira is formed from the combined rays of the third triad, Tiphareth, Netzach, and Hod. For that reason Malkuth's colors are a mixture of the colors of the preceding three spheres: citrine (Tiphareth and Netzach), olive (Netzach and Yesod), and russet brown (Hod and Yesod). A fourth color, black, is added to these three and is the result of their synthesis. Thus the colors of Malkuth are four: citrine, olive, russet brown, and black.

Malkuth's number is ten. Its titles are the Gate of Death, the Gate of the Garden of Eden, the Virgin, the Queen, the Inferior Mother, the Bride of Macroprosopos, and the Shekinah. The divine name is Adonai Ha Aretz, the Lord and King, ruling over the kingdom and empire that is the visible universe. The archangel is Sandalphon, the Prince of Prayer. The order of angels is the Ishim, or Flames of Fire, also known as the order of the Blessed Souls.

This Sephira's sphere of operation is Cholem Yesodoth, the Breaker of Foundation and the sphere of the elements, wherein all things are formed. Its telesmatic image is a young woman, crowned and throned.

Its physical correspondences are the feet and the anus. It is identified as the planet Earth.

Malkuth is essentially the sphere of humankind, of sensation. It is also the only Sephira that does not form part of a triad. It stands alone. For that reason it is seen by kabbalists as a container for the emanations of the other nine Sephiroth.

Malkuth is the seat of matter and also of the four elements of the ancients: air, fire, water, and earth. The physicist recognizes three states of matter: solid, liquid, and gas. These three forms of matter correspond to the earth, water, and air elements, respectively. The fire element corresponds to electricity. The occultist classifies all physical phenomena under these four elements in order to understand their nature.

The intrinsic quality of Malkuth is stability, the inertia of matter that is like the sway of a pendulum rhythmically oscillating throughout eternity.

Malkuth—the Earth—is a world in shadows. For it is seen not only as the world of matter but also as the world of the shells or fallen shards of the broken vessels. Another reason why the Earth is in darkness is because the Moon (Yesod) always stands between the Earth and the Sun (Tiphareth). Therefore the Sun (Tiphareth) is always in eclipse from the point of view of the Earth (Malkuth).

Malkuth is associated with the Shekinah because the Divine Bride is said to be in exile on Earth as a result of Adam's fall and the breakage of the vessels. It is therefore the mission of humanity to raise the hidden sparks of the divine light, crushed under the fallen shards, back to their initial source. Humanity can do this through its good actions, love, compassion, and all the qualities inherent in each of the Sephiroth. Only then can the Shekinah end her exile and return to her divine spouse. This process of restoration is known as *tikkun* and it is the aim of redemption. Once a human being knows the meaning and importance of tikkun, every one of his actions should be directed toward this purpose. This is particularly true of rituals and meditations whose mystical intention is known as *kavvanah*. In meditation,

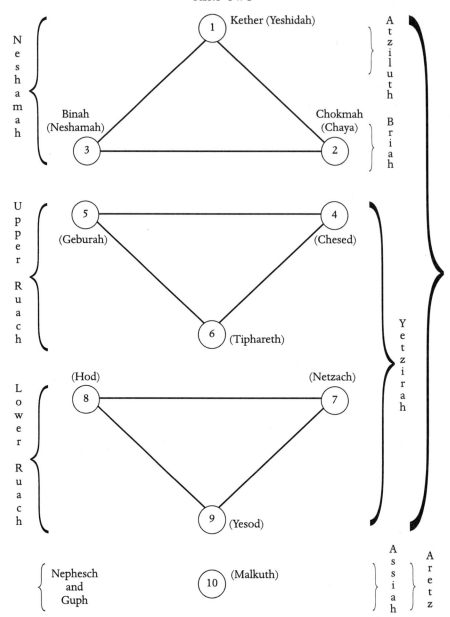

Figure 4: The Structure of the Material Body (Guph) and the Various Divisions of the Spirit (Neshamah, Upper Ruach, and Lower Ruach) in the Ten Spheres of the Tree of Life. The triangles are known as Triads and are made of nine of the Sephiroth. The tenth sphere stands by itself, as it represents the material world. The four kabbalistic worlds, Atziluth, Briah, Yetzirah, and Assiah, rule over the various divisions of the spirit and the material body.

kavvanah is used to transform the human will and make it one with God's. In this way the unity of things and the restoration of the cosmic order is accomplished.

DAATH—THE INVISIBLE SEPHIRA

Hidden halfway between the spheres of Binah and Chokmah lies an "invisible" sphere known as Daath, "knowledge."

When we refer to the scriptures and find that the physical union between a man and a woman is described as the man "knowing" the woman, we can understand the properties of Daath. An example of this is found in Genesis 4:1: "And Adam knew Eve, his wife; and she conceived and bare Cain."

The position of Daath between Chokmah and Binah, the Supernal Father and Mother, makes it obvious that the kabbalistic "secret" of their union is sex, albeit on a higher plane. Of the union between Wisdom and Understanding is born Knowledge. This knowledge, which is Daath, perceived in the material plane as the sexual union between a male and a female, is what made possible the transition of Binah from virgin (dark sterile mother) to mother (bright fertile mother).

In the archetypal world to which the three Supernals belong, the concept of Daath is not one of sex in the physical sense of the word, but of realization and illumination. It is the union of cosmic opposites for the purpose of manifestation. In the Supernal triad of Kether, Chokmah, and Binah, we have the key to our cosmogony.

Daath is placed on the Middle Pillar, between the spheres of Kether and Tiphareth. This position is important because it means that only through Knowledge—Supreme Knowledge—can a human being transcend consciousness and cross the Abyss that separates the seven lower Sephiroth from the three Supernals, which symbolize the deep unconscious or Higher Self.

The Tree of Life and the triads are also identified with the various divisions of the human spirit and the physical body (see Figure 4). The Higher Self or Neshamah is found in the first triad, composed of

Kether, Chokmah, and Binah. Neshamah is composed of three parts: Yeshidah, Chaya, and the Lower Neshamah, identified with Kether, Chokmah, and Binah, respectively. These three parts of the Higher Self are seen as cosmic gradations of the human spirit as it descends into matter from the initial spark that is God. Yeshidah is part of the first kabbalistic world, Atziluth, the World of Emanation. Chaya and the Lower Neshamah are part of the second world, Briah, the World of Creation. The three parts of Neshamah are known as the "great fire," the divine spirit in a human being.

Below Neshamah is the Ruach, or human spirit, and it represents the first breath of divine life. It is the human soul, with the first vestiges of feelings, emotions, and reason. Ruach is sometimes divided into the Upper Ruach (the second triad) and the Lower Ruach (the third triad). It falls within the aegis of the third world, Yetzirah, the World of Formation.

The animal soul, the instincts, and vital force of the human being is known as the Nephesch. The physical energy that drives the body is Kuph Ha Guph, while the physical body itself is the Guph. All three belong to the last sphere—Malkuth—identified with the Earth and the fourth world, Assiah, the World of Action.

The average human consciousness is a mixture of the Lower Ruach and the Nephesch. Unfortunately, some individuals function only through the Nephesch, of which they are veritable slaves. These are people who are driven by their instincts and most basic needs and rarely pay heed to the higher levels of their consciousness. They are like Cain, who killed his brother Abel, and when God asked him where Abel was, answered, "Am I my brother's keeper?"

The Lower Ruach deals with feelings and reason, but on a more personal level. The average person, who is concerned with the solution of his or her everyday problems, who cares about the state of society and hopes for a better world but does little about it, is functioning within the Lower Ruach but is always strongly influenced by the Nephesch.

Those persons who understand that the state of the world is part of their responsibility, who empathize with others' sorrows, and who try to alleviate society's ills through a determined and concentrated effort, are functioning within the Upper Ruach. They know that they are their brothers' keepers and act accordingly. These people are also influenced by the Nephesch but keep it well under their control. Often unknowingly, they are accomplishing the work of restoration known as tikkun, where the sparks of light hidden under the broken shells are returned to their divine origin.

Kabbalah teaches that every time we pray and ask for divine guidance, we are asking for help from our Neshamah, our Higher Self, who is also identified with our Holy Guardian Angel. All rituals and meditations, whether kabbalistic or not, which are aimed at union with the Godhead elevate the human spirit to the lofty realm of the Neshamah. People who continuously endeavor to achieve higher states of consciousness, who meditate and pray constantly and live exemplary lives, are said to function on the level of the Neshamah. This is the highest state that a human being can aspire to and is identified with the divine spark emanated from the Godhead.

6

CLIMBING THE TREE

The tree of life was also in the
midst of the garden, and the tree
of the knowledge of good and evil.

—GENESIS 2:9

As we saw in the preceding chapter, the ten Sephiroth or spheres of the Tree of Life are connected by twenty-two lines, which are known as "Paths" (see Figure 1). To each of the twenty-two Paths is ascribed one of the letters of the Hebrew alphabet. By means of these lines or Paths it is possible to "travel" or climb upon the tree. The intention is to return to God, who is symbolized by the first Sephiroth, Kether.

There are many ways to use the Paths to accomplish union with the Godhead. The simplest and fastest is directly through the Middle Pillar. This column connects Malkuth (Earth-Kingdom) to Yesod (Moon-Foundation) to Tiphareth (Sun-Beauty) to the hidden sphere Daath (Knowledge) and Kether (Crown-God). But this is also the most difficult way because it requires great purity of mind and spirit and an unflinching determination to ignore the material world in the search for the divine. This is not easy to accomplish. For that reason, kabbalists recommend "traveling" through the Paths that connect the spheres, starting from the lower Sephiroth until the higher are reached.

Each Path illuminates the human spirit through the cosmic influence of the Hebrew letter that rules it. Each letter has a specific meaning and also represents a certain number. The numbers ascribed to the letters have no mathematical significance. Each letter and each number

THE HEBREW ALPHABET

א	ב	ג	ד	ה	ו	ז	ח	ט
Aleph (A)	Beth (B)	Gimel (G)	Daleth (D)	He (H)	Vau (V)	Zayin (Z)	Cheth (CH)	Teth (T)
Ox	House	Camel	Door	Window	Peg, Nail	Weapon	Enclosure	Serpent
1	2	3	4	5	6	7	8	9
י	כ	ל	מ	נ	ס	ע	פ	צ
Yod (I)	Caph (K)	Lamed (L)	Mem (M)	Nun (N)	Samekh (S)	Ayin (O)	Pe (P)	Tzaddi (TZ)
Hand	Palm of the Hand	Ox-Goad	Water	Fish	Support	Eye	Mouth	Fishing Hook
10	20	30	40	50	60	70	80	90
ק	ר	ש	ת	ך	ם	ן	ף	ץ
Qoph (Q)	Resh (R)	Shin (SH)	Tau (TH)	Final Caph	Final Mem	Final Nun	Final Pe	Final Tzaddi
Back of the Head	Head	Tooth	Sign of the Cross					
100	200	300	400	500	600	700	800	900

Table 4.

is simply an ideogram, a symbol of a cosmic force. The interaction between these cosmic energies is taking place simultaneously in the universe as well as in humanity.

The Kabbalah teaches that God created the universe by means of the Hebrew alphabet. The twenty-two letters that form the alphabet are really twenty-two different states of consciousness of the cosmic energy, and are the essence of all that exists. Although they represent numbers, symbols, and ideas, they cannot be easily classified because they are virtually all the things they designate. Our ordinary languages are sensually derived; that is, they have been designed to express our sensory perceptions, what we see, touch, hear. The word *house* in English means "dwelling," the same as *casa* in Spanish or *haus* in German. But in Hebrew, the letter Beth means more than house. It is the essence of house. It is the archetype of all dwellings or containers. Each letter of the Hebrew alphabet is a cosmic archetype of its meaning and its number (see Table 4).

Aleph (1), Beth (2), Gimel (3), Daleth (4), He (5), Vau (6), Zayin (7), Cheth (8), and Teth (9) are the archetypes of numbers 1 to 9. These first nine letters project themselves into higher stages of manifestations by the addition of zeroes. The next series of letters from Yod (10) to Tzaddi (90) are exalted states of the first nine letters. The third series, from Qoph (100) to Final Tzaddi (900), represent the highest cosmic states.

The cosmic and material meaning of the letters and the Path of the Tree they represent is as follows:

1. **Aleph**—archetypal number 1. *Cosmic:* The dual principle that represents all that exists and all that does not exist, the positive and negative, life and death. *Material:* Guide, creation, direction, impulse. Its symbol is an ox. Path 11, connecting the first and second Sephiroth, Kether and Chokmah.

2. **Beth**—archetypal number 2. *Cosmic:* The symbol of all habitations and receptacles, of anything that "contains." *Material:* Protection, insurance, survival. Its symbol is a house. Path 12, connecting the first and third Sephiroth, Kether and Binah.

3. **Gimel**—archetypal number 3. *Cosmic:* The activity, the motion of contained, limited existence or nonexistence, Aleph in Beth. *Material:* Realization, splendor, possessions. Its symbol is a camel. Path 13, connecting the first and sixth Sephiroth, Kether and Tiphareth.

4. **Daleth**—archetypal number 4. *Cosmic:* The archetype of physical existence. *Material:* Justice, law, foundation, point of entry. Its symbol is a door. Path 14, connecting the second and third Sephiroth, Chokmah and Binah, and traversing Daath, the hidden sphere.

5. **He**—archetypal number 5. *Cosmic:* The principle of universal life. *Material:* Life, love, warmth, reproduction. Its symbol is a window. Path 15, connecting the second and sixth Sephiroth, Chokmah and Tiphareth.

6. **Vau**—archetypal number 6. *Cosmic:* The archetype of all fertilizing substances. *Material:* Union, association, dependency, relationships. Its symbol is a nail. Path 16, connecting the second and fourth Sephiroth, Chokmah and Chesed.

7. **Zayin**—archetypal number 7. *Cosmic:* The completed fertilizing act. *Material:* Force, violence, potency, outpouring. Its symbol is a weapon. Path 17, connecting the third and sixth Sephiroth, Binah and Tiphareth.

8. **Cheth**—archetypal number 8. *Cosmic:* The enclosure of all unevolved cosmic energy. *Material:* Concentration, groupings, gathering of things. Its symbol is an enclosure. Path 18, connecting the third and the fifth Sephiroth, Binah and Geburah.

9. **Teth**—archetypal number 9. *Cosmic:* The symbol of the initial female energy. *Material:* Wisdom, reflection, prudence. Its symbol is a serpent. Path 19, connecting the fourth and fifth Sephiroth, Chesed and Geburah.

10. **Yod**—archetypal number 10. *Cosmic:* A steady-state continuity. *Material:* Cause, perfection, power, pressure, generation. Its symbol is a hand. Path 20, connecting the fourth and the sixth Sephiroth, Chesed and Tiphareth.

11. **Caph**—archetypal number 20. *Cosmic:* The archetype of all receivers. *Material:* Purity, offering, generosity. Its symbol is the palm of the hand. Path 21, connecting the fourth and seventh Sephiroth, Chesed and Netzach.

12. **Lamed**—archetypal number 30. *Cosmic:* The principle of the conscious, connecting link. *Material:* Learning, sacrifice, dedica-

tion. Its symbol is the ox-goad. Path 22, connecting the fifth and sixth Sephiroth, Geburah and Tiphareth.

13. **Mem**—archetypal number 40. *Cosmic:* The archetype of the maternal creative principle. *Material:* Fertility, replication, variation. Its symbol is water. Path 23, connecting the fifth and eighth Sephiroth, Geburah and Hod.

14. **Nun**—archetypal number 50. *Cosmic:* The archetype of all individual existences. *Material:* Expansion, propagation, children, growth, increase. Its symbol is a fish. Path 24, connecting the sixth and seventh Sephiroth, Tiphareth and Netzach.

15. **Samekh**—archetypal number 60. *Cosmic:* The archetype of female fertility, the ovum. *Material:* Sustenance, shrewdness, repetition, knowledge. Its symbol is support. Path 25, connecting the sixth and ninth Sephiroth, Tiphareth and Yesod.

16. **Ayin**—archetypal number 70. *Cosmic:* The illuminating principle behind the act of impregnation. *Material:* Understanding, source, attention, extension, prevention. Its symbol is the eye. Path 26, connecting the sixth Sephiroth, Tiphareth and Hod.

17. **Pe**—archetypal number 80. *Cosmic:* The same as Cheth, that is, the enclosure of all unevolved cosmic energy. *Material:* Explanation, mandate, language, power of speech. Its symbol is the mouth. Path 27, connecting the seventh and eighth Sephiroth, Netzach and Hod.

18. **Tzaddi**—archetypal number 90. *Cosmic:* The symbol of womanhood in a social sense. *Material:* Control, assurance, expansion. Its symbol is a fishing hook. Path 28, connecting the seventh and the ninth Sephiroth, Netzach and Yesod.

19. **Qoph**—archetypal number 100. *Cosmic:* An exalted state of Aleph, transcending the negative or death aspect. *Material:* Repose, period, cycle. Its symbol is the back of the head. Path 29,

connecting the seventh and tenth Sephiroth, Netzach and Malkuth.

20. **Resh**—archetypal number 200. *Cosmic:* The archetype of universal or cosmic containers, a higher state of Beth. *Material:* Intelligence, ideas, perspicacity, intellectual grasp. Its symbol is the head. Path 30, connecting the eighth and ninth Sephiroth, Hod and Yesod.

21. **Shin**—archetypal number 300. *Cosmic:* The "spirit" of God. *Material:* Transformation, nature, change, renovation. Its symbol is a tooth. Path 31, connecting the eighth and tenth Sephiroth, Hod and Malkuth.

22. **Tau**—archetypal number 400. *Cosmic:* The archetype of all cosmic existence. *Material:* Identity, death, plenitude, return, sign. Its symbol is a quail. Path 32, connecting the ninth and tenth Sephiroth, Yesod and Malkuth.

Final Caph—archetypal number 500. *Cosmic:* The cosmic final attainment of individual existences. *Material:* High achievements, success, triumph on every level. No Path.

Final Mem—archetypal number 600. *Cosmic:* The cosmic fertility in humankind, both in mind and body. *Material:* Brilliancy of intellect, intellectual achievements, happy family life. No Path.

Final Nun—archetypal number 700. *Cosmic:* The symbol of the interplay of cosmic energies. *Material:* Success in both the professional and personal life. No Path.

Final Pe—archetypal number 800. *Cosmic:* The same as Pe and Cheth. *Material:* Success in government and worldly affairs. No Path.

Final Tzaddi—archetypal number 900. *Cosmic:* The archetype of womanhood in a mythical sense. *Material:* Success in all things connected with women's affairs. No Path.

As explained earlier, the ten Sephiroth are the first ten Paths of the tree. That is why the letters begin with Path 11 and end with Path 32. You will note that the letters and their Paths begin on the top of the tree, connecting all the various Sephiroth in descending order. The sixth and central Sephira—Tiphareth—has the most Paths, eight in total. The reason for this is that Tiphareth represents the Sun and therefore receives light from the Divine Source, Kether, and shares this light with all the other spheres, which are identified with the planets of the solar system, as well as the Moon. As we saw earlier, the Earth does not receive light from the Sun in the Tree of Life because the Moon (Yesod) creates a spiritual eclipse, standing as it does between the Earth (Malkuth) and the Sun (Tiphareth). That is why our world is said to be in darkness. For that reason, the first Path that should be "traveled" in the ascent through the tree should be Path 32, connecting the tenth and ninth Sephiroth. This Path is identified with the letter Tau, which represents the archetype of all cosmic existence as well as Death and Plenitude. Death in this context means not only the physical and eventual death of the human body, but the "death" of all material desires. When this spiritual Death of matter is achieved, the individual reaches the Plenitude of illumination. He is then able to banish the darkness of Malkuth and receives in return the silvery light of the Moon of Yesod.

The cosmic and material meanings of the letters can be applied to each of the twenty-two Paths to which they are connected. Meditation on each individual Path and the spheres that it connects gives the individual a profound understanding of both the spiritual and the material aspects of the Sephiroth.

As we saw earlier, each Sephira represents different human endeavors and interests. When a person desires to obtain spiritual and material knowledge about a specific situation or problem in his life, he chooses the Sephira that represents it and ascends through the tree via the appropriate Paths until he reaches that Sephira. He must always start from the tenth sphere, Malkuth, which represents him as well as the material plane. He then finds the connecting Paths and meditates

HUMAN ENDEAVORS IN THE TREE OF LIFE

Sephira	Human Endeavor
1. Kether	None
2. Chokmah	None
3. Binah	None
4. Chesed	Growth, journeys, banks, debts, gambling, abundance
5. Geburah	Dangers, surgery, construction, destruction, war
6. Tiphareth	Success, money, power, superiors, mental power
7. Netzach	Love, passion, women, arts, music, pleasure, enjoyment
8. Hod	Papers, books, business matters, contracts
9. Yesod	Affairs of women, the mother, changes, moves, short trips
10. Malkuth	Where energies are gathered

NATURAL CORRESPONDENCES
OF THE TREE OF LIFE

Sephira	Plant	Animal	Incense	Metal	Stone
1. Kether	almond flower	———	ambergris	———	diamond
2. Chokmah	amaranth	man	musk	———	ruby, turquoise
3. Binah	cypress, poppy	woman	myrrh, civet	lead	sapphire
4. Chesed	olive, shamrock	unicorn	cedar	tin	amethyst
5. Geburah	oak	basilisk	tobacco	iron	ruby
6. Tiphareth	acacia, bay, vine	lion	olibanum	gold	topaz
7. Netzach	rose	lynx	benzoin, rose	copper	emerald
8. Hod	moly	hermaphrodite	storax	quicksilver	opal
9. Yesod	mandrake, damiana	elephant	jasmine	silver	white quartz
10. Malkuth	lily, ivy	sphinx	Dittany of Crete	mica	rock crystal

Table 5, top, and 6, bottom.

on their meanings. When he reaches the Sephira he is interested in, he lingers there, meditating on its specific meanings, and then he must establish a connection with the opposite Sephira in order to "balance" the tree. That means crossing the Path that connects both spheres and meditating on the opposite sphere as well. The only spheres that do not need to be balanced are Tiphareth, Yesod, and Malkuth, as they stand alone on the Middle Pillar.

Tables 1–3 and Tables 5 and 6 give the various correspondences of each Sephira, including colors, stones, metals, incenses, numbers, human endeavors, and the names of God, the archangels and the angelic orders assigned to them. Table 7 gives the colors of the Paths and the Hebrew letters. This information is necessary during meditation on the tree. The colors of the Sephiroth upon which one meditates and the colors of the Paths that lead to them must be carefully visualized and concentrated on during the ascension on the tree, as well as the letters and their meanings. The name of the aspect of God that rules the spheres and the names of the archangels and angelic orders must also be pronounced and meditated upon.

There are four different color scales related to the tree, one for each of the four kabbalistic worlds which, as we have seen, are Atziluth (World of Emanation), Briah (World of Creation), Yetzirah (World of Formation), and Assiah (World of Action). The color scale used during meditation on the tree is the Briatic scale corresponding to the World of Creation. This scale was chosen by kabbalists because it pertains to the world where ideas were first evolved (see Table 2).

Kabbalah stresses the importance of balance on the tree because the powerful energies of the Sephiroth, when unbalanced, can create turmoil and destruction. When the cosmic energy was first flowing from Kether to Chokmah, its force was not fully stabilized, for it still lacked form and direction. This surplus of energy overflowed and spilled downward, creating ten adverse Sephiroth known as the Qlippoth. These negative spheres coalesced on Malkuth, which became their first Sephira. Therefore we have a second Tree, chaotic and unbalanced,

COLORS OF THE PATHS
AND THE HEBREW LETTERS

Path	Color	Hebrew Letter
11	sky blue	Aleph
12	purple	Beth
13	silver	Gimel
14	sky blue	Daleth
15	bright red	Heh
16	deep indigo	Vau
17	pale mauve	Zayin
18	maroon	Cheth
19	deep purple	Teth
20	slate grey	Yod
21	medium blue	Caph
22	medium blue	Lamed
23	sea-green	Mem
24	dull brown	Nun
25	yellow	Samekh
26	black	Ayin
27	tomato red	Peh
28	sky blue	Tzaddi
29	beige flecked with silvery white	Qoph
30	gold yellow	Resh
31	vermillion	Shin
32	dark purple	Tau

The colors given in this table are from the Briah scale. Paths 11 to 32 connect the ten spheres of the Tree of Life. Paths 1 to 10 are represented by the spheres themselves.

Table 7.

which begins at Malkuth and extends downwards towards the Abyss. These ten Sephiroth are the complete opposites of the harmonious forces that form the Tree of Life. As such they are considered evil and are identified with the infernal regions.

The Qlippoth are not independent principles in the cosmic scale, but the unbalanced and destructive aspects of the spheres of the Tree of Life. Therefore there are two trees, and they both must be taken into consideration for the proper understanding of the kabbalistic doctrine. For wherever there is a virtue or a positive Sephira, there is a corresponding vice, which is symbolized by the adverse Qlippoth.

The two trees, Sephirotic and Qlippothic, are often represented as if the infernal spheres—which are on the reverse side of the divine ones, like the opposite sides of a coin—were a reflection of the Tree of Life, from a mirror placed at its base. In this concept, the Qlippoth seem to extend downward from the sphere of Malkuth, where they abut. Malkuth, according to tradition, is a fallen Sephira, for it was separated from the rest of the tree by Adam's Fall. Thus the material world rests upon the infernal one known also as the "shells." That is the reason why their influence is felt so strongly in human affairs.

The demons of the Qlippoth are the most unbalanced and chaotic of all principles. The first two spheres of the Qlippothic tree, corresponding inversely to Kether and Chokmah, are void and disorganized, while the third sphere, corresponding to Binah, is known as the abode of darkness. Then follow what are called the seven tabernacles—Shebah Hekoles—or so-called hell, which shows us in a systematic outline all the disorders of the moral world and all the torments consequent to them. There may be found every negative feeling of the human heart, every vice, every crime, and every weakness personified in a demon who becomes the tormentor of those led astray by these faults.

The seven infernal tabernacles are divided and subdivided ad infinitum; for every kind of perversity there is a special "kingdom" and thus the Abyss unfolds itself gradually in all its depth and immensity. The supreme chief of that world of darkness is Samael, the angel of poison and death. He is identified with the biblical Satan. Samael is given two wives, Isheh Zenunim and Lilith, who is the personification of vice and sensuality. From his union with Lilith springs the Beast, Chiva, often represented as a goat with female breasts. Lilith is said to be behind the death of all infants, as she takes great pleasure in the destruction of childhood and innocence.

From the preceding discussion we see that the Qlippoth are the result of the unbalanced surplus energy that gave rise to the Sephiroth of the Tree of Life. This unbalanced force forms the center around which revolve all the evil thoughtforms of humanity. It is therefore the source as well as the consequence of all evil thoughts and actions. Because the Qlippoth were evolved from an overflow of cosmic energy, their influence is directly related to excess in any form. Thus an excess of love gives rise to jealousy and possessiveness, an excess in sexual desire gives rise to lust, an excess of worldly ambition gives rise to avarice, until all the gamut of human qualities and inspirations are debased and vilified. That is the reason why Kabbalah places such a great importance on the perfect balance of the energies of the Sephiroth.

We saw earlier that the fastest method to ascend the tree is through the Middle Pillar. This method is used only by the true mystic, who wishes to acquire illumination or the same thing, which is to establish a perfect equilibrium within his personality and a total harmony with the soul of the universe. This method is known as the Path of the Arrow, which is shot from the "bow of promise," Quesheth, the rainbow of astral colors that spreads like a halo behind Yesod. This system does not confer any "magical" powers and is used by the mystic to rise from the material plane to the higher planes of exalted consciousness. It is called the Path of the Arrow because it moves in a straight line from Malkuth to Kether. The process is conducted mainly through meditation upon the letters, the colors, the divine names, and the symbols associated with the Sephiroth and the Paths connecting these spheres.

A second method used by kabbalists as a meditation system is known as the Flash of Lightning. It is likened to the coils of a serpent that extend in zigzag throughout the tree, traversing its whole length, Sephira by Sephira. Unlike the Path of the Arrow, which is an ascending Path, the Flash of Lightning is used for the "descent of power" (see Figure 5, next page). In this system the kabbalist concentrates on Kether, the first sphere, using the divine names and the appropriate symbols, and then brings down that power through the remaining spheres, again using the names and symbols, all the way down to Malkuth, which represents him and the world of matter. There he gathers the cosmic energy of the Flash of Lightning and absorbs it into himself. He does this through meditation and breathing exercises.

Another system, known as Rising on the Planes, uses a reverse form of the Flash of Lightning. In this method the person starts from Malkuth and traverses all the spheres in zigzag form until he reaches Kether. In this system he elevates his consciousness by contacting the ten Sephiroth.

As a meditation system the Tree of Life is of immense value, not only to the kabbalist, but to anyone who desires to harmonize the cosmic forces that form the structure of his soul. For we must remember that each Sephira represents the purest essence of a human quality or virtue. If we absorb the tree into our souls, we are harmonizing ourselves with the divine aspects of those qualities and virtues. This is the highest and purest aim of practical work on the Tree of Life.

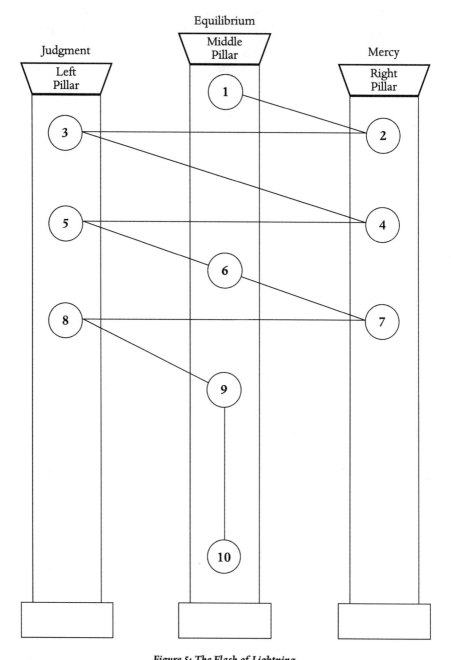

Figure 5: The Flash of Lightning.
The Flash of Lightning depicts the descent of cosmic energy as it pours down from the first to the tenth Sephira of the Tree of Life.

7

LETTERS OF LIGHT

Then God said, "Let there be
light," and there was light.

—GENESIS 1:3

"In the beginning there was light, and plenty of it," said astrophysicist George Gamow. He was referring to the event known as the Big Bang, the most accepted scientific theory on the origins of the universe. It was Gamow who presented the concept of the Big Bang in 1956 to the scientific community. According to this theory, about fifteen billion years ago, the universe was compressed into a single point of light. This point, known as a singularity, was all that existed at the beginning of creation. The point of light continued to contract until it burst in an ineffable explosion, creating not only fundamental subatomic particles, and thus matter and energy, but space and time itself. In the first three minutes following the explosion, the new cosmos went through a superfast inflation, expanding from the size of an atomic nucleus to the size of a grapefruit. At this point space was a seething "hot soup" of subatomic particles too hot to form into atoms. Charged electrons and protons prevented light from shining through the dense fog scattered throughout the newly created space. In the next three hundred thousand years, electrons and protons combined to form the first atom, that of hydrogen, the fundamental basis of creation. Light could finally shine (see Hawking, *Brief History of Time*).

The hydrogen atoms combined to form helium. In the next billion years, gravity made hydrogen and helium coalesce to form the giant clouds that would later become galaxies. Smaller clumps of gas collapsed to form the first stars. As galaxies clustered together under gravity, the first stars died, spewing heavy new elements into space. These eventually formed into new stars and planets.

Interstellar gases and stars emit microwave radiation. In 1965 scientists Arno Penzias and Robert Wilson from the Bell Telephone Laboratories detected microwave background radiation that could be traced back to the time of the Big Bang. This finding earned them a Nobel Prize and proved the validity of the Big Bang theory (see Hawking, *Universe in a Nutshell*).

The singularity or point of light that began the Big Bang can be easily equated with the Ain Soph at the moment of creation. The long period of cosmic evolution that transpired between the initial point of light and the creation of Earth was a simultaneous occurrence for the Ain Soph, for whom time does not exist. As we have seen, time and space came into being at the time of the Big Bang. Therefore Ain Soph exists outside time and space.

Light is a form of radiant energy that has no mass and no electrical charge, but can create photons and electrons, the building blocks of the atom and thus of the universe. According to Planck's Quantum Theory, light is transmitted in "whole pieces" or *quanta* of action, also known as photons (see Gamow, *Thirty Years That Shook Physics*). These whole pieces of action are nonphysical and yet are the basis of the physical world. And despite the abhorrence that teleology, or purposive design in nature, awakens in scientists, the photon or unit of light seems to be motivated by a definite purpose. In the words of Planck, "photons . . . behave like intelligent human beings." This observed phenomenon is known as the principle of action or least action. It was also Planck who said that the development of theoretical physics has led to the formulation of the principle of physical causality that is explicitly teleological in character. In other words, physics has proved that there is a definite purpose behind the causes of the material world, which is something that the ancient kabbalists knew before the advent of physics.

The theory of relativity presented to the world a new, fascinating fact about the properties of light, namely that time does not exist in the world of photons. Clocks stop at the speed of light. Even space is

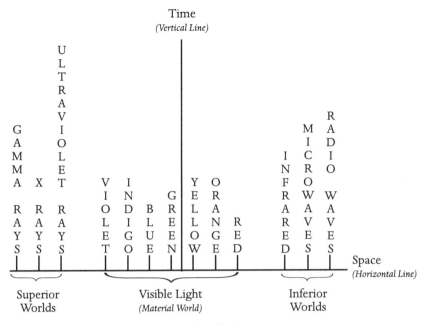

Figure 6: The Solar Spectrum.
The seven visible colors of the material world are in the middle of the spectrum. Yellow is
the first of the three primary colors (yellow, red, and blue), as it gives rise to the secondary
colors, green and orange, through its blending with blue and red. The cosmic rays on the
right of the spectrum (infrared, microwaves, and radio waves) are identified with the inferior worlds as they create distraction, noise, and confusion. The rays on the left (ultraviolet,
X rays, and gamma rays) are associated with the superior worlds as they nourish, heal, and
transcend the material plane. The horizontal line (space), where it is dissected by the vertical line (time), represents the present. To the right of the Time line lies the past, and to the
left is the future.

an insignificant concept for light because photons can travel through
space without any loss of energy. Furthermore, light cannot be really
"seen." It simply makes seeing possible. Einstein showed that time is
the fourth dimension, supplementing the three coordinates of space:
width, length, and depth. He combined space and time to establish a
space-time continuum using the speed of light as a link between the
time and space dimensions (see Einstein, *Relativity*). Space may be seen
as a horizontal line extending itself throughout infinity. Time may be
seen as a vertical line dissecting the line of space to create reality as we
know it. Along the line of space may be found the various electromagnetic radiations that include visible light (see Figure 6).

All the characteristics that science has attributed to light are remarkably similar to those that the kabbalists, who see God as light, attribute to God. And if we also take into consideration that, according to Planck, there is a definite purpose behind physical causality, we can say, without stretching either the truth or the imagination, that science has proven the existence of God.

From the preceding we can see that the kabbalistic concept of God as light agrees in principle with the concept of light as presented by science. We also have seen that time does not "exist" for light. That means that all events must exist together, before and after their manifestation, in the world of light. All given moments must exist simultaneously and may be in contact with one another, even when divided by great intervals of time. Thus for God, who is light, all time processes blend together into an infinite sequence of events. This provides a valid basis for the reconciliation of the creation of the universe with the Darwinian theory of the Origin of Species.

The long process of evolution, which for humanity is measured in millions of years, was a simultaneous occurrence for God. Moreover, science "recognizes" six stages in the creation of the universe. Genesis says that "the earth was without form and void." Science tells us that in the beginning the material out of which Earth was formed was scattered in utter chaos throughout the original nebula. According to Genesis, God says, "Let there be light and there was light." Science states that the initial atoms were set in motion throughout the nebula, giving rise to light. This was the "first stage." Genesis says that the firmament was created during the second day. Science says that during the "second stage," the Earth settled down into a spherical shape and the atmosphere (the firmament) was formed. Genesis speaks of the creation of land and water on the third day. Science says that in the "third stage," while the atmosphere was still dense, the waters began to settle in the low places. While Genesis speaks of the creation of the Sun, the Moon, and the stars on the fourth day, science says that the atmosphere thinned out, letting the Sun, the Moon, and the stars be seen. Genesis says that God created the sea creatures on the fifth day. Science says

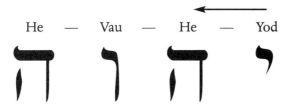

He — Vau — He — Yod

Figure 7: *The most holy name of God, Yod He Vau He,*
also known as the Tetragrammaton (Great Name of Four Letters).
It is sometimes pronounced as *Yaweh* or *Jehovah*, but both pronunciations are incorrect according to Hebrew scholars. The twenty-two Hebrew letters are consonants. The vowel sounds are indicated by a series of small dots under some of the letters. These dots are missing in the Tetragrammaton, purposely erased by the ancients so that the correct pronunciation of the holiest of names would be hidden from the profane. In ancient times the name was pronounced once a year by the High Priest of the temple. In modern times no one knows (or admits to know) the correct pronunciation. The name is read from right to left, as indicated by the arrow.

that the first sign of life on Earth took place in the oceans. Genesis says that God created cattle and man on the sixth day. Science tells us that mammals were among the last species to be developed on Earth.

As we have seen, according to the Kabbalah, God used the letter Beth to create the universe. This letter represents the essence of all containers. What God "contained" though the power of Beth was a ray of his infinite light. All the letters of the Hebrew alphabet, like Beth, are cosmic principles and as such they are all purveyors of God's light.

We saw in chapter 3 that God has many names and that the holiest of these names is the Tetragrammaton, which we better know as Jehovah, the Lord God. This name is made of four letters: Yod, He, Vau, He (see Figure 7). The letter Yod's cosmic meaning is steady-state continuity. The letter He represents the principle of universal life and love. Vau is the archetype of all fertilizing substances. We know from chapter 3 that it was Jehovah—the Lord God—who created Adam and Eve. The meaning of the letters of the holiest of God's name reveals that through a continuous process (Yod), the Creator emanated the principle of universal life identified as love (He), granting it the gift of fertility (Vau). But because there are two *He*'s in the name, the principle of universal life was emanated twice. These two principles of life are a male and a female (Adam and Eve) who are fertile and able to multiply. The creation was continuous because God emanates his light perennially in order to sustain the world.

The Tetragrammaton—Yod He Vau He—is commonly transliterated as IHVH. Its intrinsic meaning is "to be," and it is a symbol of existence. It also represents the four cardinal points, the four stations, the four elements (air, fire, water, and earth), and the four worlds of the kabbalists, among other things. The name may be transposed in twelve different ways, all of which mean "to be." The twelve transpositions are known as the Twelve Banners of the Mighty Name and are said to represent the twelve signs of the zodiac. They are IHVH, IHHV, IVHH, HVHI, HVIH, HHIV, VHHI, VIHH, VHIH, HIHV, HIVH, HHVI.

God has three other four-letter names which are: AHIH, pronounced *Eheieh* (Existence); ADNI, pronounced *Adonai* (Lord), and AGLA. This last name is a composition of the first letters of the words of the following sentence: *Atoh Gebor Leolahm Adonai* (Thou are mighty forever, O Lord). This is based on the kabbalistic code system known as Notarikon. There are two forms of Notarikon. In the first, every letter of a word is used to start another word until a whole sentence is formed based on the original word. For example, from the word GLINT we can create the following sentence: God Lives In Nature's Tabernacles. The second form of Notarikon, used in AGLA, is the exact opposite of the first. From the initial or final letters of a sentence, a word or name is formed.

The similarities between IHVH (Jehovah) and AHIH (Eheieh) are very marked. To begin with, they are both symbols of existence. Also, the letter He (H), the archetype of universal life, is the second and fourth character in both names. Kabbalistically, AHIH is the unmanifested cosmic principle, God before creation, while IHVH is the manifested cosmic principle, the creation itself. AHIH is the name that the Creator gave to Moses from the burning bush: *Eheieh Asher Eheieh*, that is, I AM THAT I AM. It is composed of the Hebrew letters Aleph, He,

Yod, and He. Eheieh is also the divine name ascribed to the first Sephira of the Tree of Life. It is only when Eheieh sends the flow of divine light from Kether to Chokmah that creation truly begins. The divine name in Chokmah is Yah, composed of the last two letters of Eheieh, Yod and He. When the divine energy flows from the male principle, Chokmah, to the female principle, Binah, the divine name in this third Sephira becomes Jehovah Elohim. It is the union of the male and the female cosmic principles for the purpose of manifestation. From this moment onward creation comes into being in the physical sense of the word.

We have seen that each Hebrew letter is also a number. Beth, the letter that God used to create the universe, also represents number two. Kabbalah teaches that this number is of deep significance because it symbolizes duality, which is ever present throughout the universe. Everything in the cosmos is based on the perfect balance of two principles: positive and negative, masculine and feminine. The perfect example of this duality is our modern binary system. Our highly technological society depends on the binary system for its perfect functioning. Every aspect of our daily lives has been computerized, and computers are binary programmed. Every bill, every bank statement, every hospital stay, every airplane flight, every market flow, every form of media, including entertainment—in fact, everything—is computer based. And the computer does not understand anything that is not expressed in binary form.

The binary system revolves around two cyphers, one and zero, the all and the nothing. The electronic circuits used in this technology are known as two-state or bi-stable. This means that only two states of electromagnetic energy are possible, as exemplified by the On and the Off switches of electrical outlets. "On" means that electricity is pulsating through the system and the circuit is open. "Off" means that the electricity is not flowing and the circuit is closed. The On in the electric system corresponds to the one in the binary system. The Off corresponds to the zero. Every computer program is recognized only as combinations of ones and zeroes by digital computers.

The numbers that we commonly know—1, 2, 3, 4, 5, 6, 7, 8, 9 and 0—are found in the decimal system. Any number in the decimal system may be transformed into the binary system by dividing it by two until nothing remains. Kabbalah uses the decimal system but adds zeroes to the values of the letters to indicate higher states of cosmic or divine energy. We can see from Table 4 that the letters, including the final ones, are placed in rows from one to nine. In the first line we have the first nine letters with their corresponding numbers. In the second line we see the same numbers with an added zero. In the third line two zeroes have been added to the numerals one to nine. The first letter that gets a zero is Yod, making it number ten. It is interesting that Yod is also the tenth of the twenty-second letters of the Hebrew alphabet. Yod is the first letter of God's holiest name, Yod He Vau He (IHVH). It is no coincidence that it is the letter formed by the two cyphers of the binary system. Yod is steady-state continuity. It is the constant flow of radiant energy from which the universe was created. It is the universe, a universe based on a polarity made of ones and zeroes.

Every divine name has a number formed by the added value of its letters. The combined sum of Yod He Vau He is 26. That number is reached by adding Yod (10), He (5), Vau (6) and He (5). To change this decimal number into the binary system we must divide it by two until it can no longer be reduced. Let us do that now.

26 divided by 2 = 13 and the remnant is 0

13 divided by 2 = 6 and the remnant is 1

6 divided by 2 = 3 and the remnant is 0

3 divided by 2 = 1 and the remnant is 1

1 divided by 2 =0 and the remnant is 1

The remnants are the binary number of twenty-six. This number is 01011. But there is an interesting fact about binary numbers. They must be read from right to left. That means that the correct binary number for Yod He Vau He is 11010. It is interesting to note in this context that Hebrew words, as in the binary system, are read from right to left. In Hebrew the Tetragrammaton is written He Vau He Yod (see Figure 7). But when it is read from right to left it becomes Yod He Vau He.

The Tetragrammaton's binary number begins with 1 and ends with 0. These two cyphers form 10, the number of Yod. Let us look at creation in the light of Yod He Vau He's binary number, 11010. In the beginning, God sends the first ray of light symbolized by the first 1. But the spheres where the light is contained break through the force of the divine power. God then sends another ray of light, the second 1, and creation is established. God then withdraws, symbolized by the 0, and what remains are the third 1 and the last 0, representing the 10 spheres of the Tree of Life.

Pythagoras said, "Nature geometrizes." Geometry is a system that combines letters and numbers. Calculus does the same thing, giving each letter a numerical value. Kabbalah reduces everything to numbers. Gematria is a kabbalistic code system where words with the same numerical values are considered identical to each other. For example, the words *achad* (unity) and *ahebah* (love) both add up to thirteen. They are therefore considered to be one and the same.

From all of this can be seen that God created the universe based on numbers represented by the Hebrew letters. These numbers, encoded in the letter Beth, are dual in nature; they are two, the binary cyphers one and zero.

God is light, says the Kabbalah. Light is a form of electromagnetic radiation. This can be described as a stream of photons, massless particles traveling in a wavelike pattern and moving at the speed of light, 186,000 per second. Each photon contains a certain amount (or bundle) of energy, and all electromagnetic radiation consists of these photons. The only difference between the various types of electromagnetic radiation is the amount of energy found in the photons. In order to understand this better we must look at the electromagnetic spectrum (see Figure 6). You can see from this figure that electromagnetic radiation is divided into "visible" light—the seven colors of refracted "white" light—and several other types of radiation.

A prism will separate white light into seven colors: red, orange, yellow, green, blue, indigo, and violet. When passing through a prism, the wavelengths of light are bent or refracted to varying degrees. Violet light is bent the most and red light is bent the least. That is why they are at opposite ends of the solar spectrum. You will note that yellow is at the center of the spectrum. Orange is between red and yellow and is a combination of both. On the other side of yellow is the color green, which is a combination of the yellow and blue lights. They are followed by indigo and violet. Rainbows are an example of the refraction of light. Of these seven, red, yellow, and blue are primary colors. All other colors are combinations of these three. Red, yellow, and blue combine to form white light. White reflects all colors. Black absorbs them. For that reason we can say that black is the absence of color, and white contains every color.

When we combine red and indigo we obtain violet. From this we can see that the line of the spectrum, showing the seven colors, bends upon itself and forms a circle, thereby uniting red and indigo to form violet.

Beyond the color red we have infrared radiation. We often think of this as heat because it makes our skin feel warm. In space, infrared maps the dust between stars. After infrared comes microwave radiation. This will cook our food in record time but in space it is used by astronomers to learn about the structure of faraway galaxies, including our own Milky Way. As we saw earlier, microwave radiation proved the validity of the Big Bang theory. The next form of electromagnetic radiation is radio. This is the same kind of energy that radio and television stations emit into the airwaves. But it is also emitted by stars and gases in space, letting us know what they are made of.

Beyond the color violet there is ultraviolet radiation. The Sun is a source of ultraviolet rays but stars and other "hot" objects in space also emit ultraviolet radiation. After ultraviolet come X rays. Doctors use them to look inside our bodies, but the greatest source of X rays come from hot gases in outer space. Lastly we have the gamma rays. Radioactive materials, some natural and some man-made in nuclear power plants and particle accelerators, can emit gamma rays. But the biggest gamma-ray generator is the universe itself.

Astronomers have been able to detect gamma-ray bursts, sources of energy so intense as to exceed by many times the total energy of an exploding supernova. Several years ago, they discovered a gamma-ray burst so brilliant that it was brighter than the rest of the observable universe. This brightness meant that the event was more energetic than any other to date, with the exception of the Big Bang, the explosion that occurred at the very beginning of the universe. They theorized that this event could have been caused by the collision of two large black holes. Nothing else could explain a burst of radiant energy of such magnitude. This cataclysmic happening took place twelve billion light years from Earth. The fact that the burst was brighter than the observable universe and that it could be seen from a distance of twelve billion light years gives us an idea of the awesome power of gamma rays. Astronomers believe that a gamma burst occurring less than six million years away from Earth would disintegrate our planet (as was determined by Fishman in his Burst and Transient Source Experiment).

In more recent years, some astronomers have advanced the theory that there is an immense source of gamma rays around the center of the universe. The radiant energy emitted by this source is so incalculable it staggers the imagination. Could this source be the light emitted by the Ain Soph?

KEYS OF THE KINGDOM

8

THE KING ON A CROSS

And he bearing his cross went forth
into a place called the place of a skull,
which is called in the Hebrew Golgotha.

—JOHN 19:17

Jesus Christ was executed on a Roman cross two thousand years ago. He died, was buried and, after three days, rose from the dead. This belief is the cornerstone of the Christian faith, and has transformed the course of human history. But why? What really happened?

Crucifixion probably first began among the Persians. The Greek historian Herodotus tells us that King Darius had three thousand Babylonians crucified around 519 BC (see Herodotus, *Histories*). Alexander the Great also used crucifixion in his conquests and introduced it to Egypt and Carthage. Romans appeared to have learned of its usage through the Carthaginians. The Assyrians, the Scythians, and the Celts, and later on the German tribes and the Britons, also used crucifixion as a means of execution.

The Persians would tie the condemned person to a tree or impale him on an upright post to keep his feet from touching holy ground. Later a true cross was used, characterized by an upright post (*stipes*) and a horizontal beam (*patibulum*). There were several variations. Archaeological and historical evidence strongly indicates that the Tau cross was preferred by the Romans in Palestine at the time of Jesus. The upright post of this cross ends at the crossbeam and does not have the short extension above the head. But since crucifixion practices often varied in different geographic locations, the Latin cross and other forms also may have been used.

Although Romans did not invent the crucifixion, they perfected it as a form of torture and execution designed to cause a slow death with a maximum of pain and suffering. The ancients considered crucifixion the most shameful, painful, and vile of all executions. The Roman statesman Cicero called it "the most cruel and disgusting extreme penalty" (see Cicero, *Selected Works*). The Jewish historian Josephus, who witnessed many crucifixions, called it "the most wretched of deaths" (see Josephus, *Works*). Seneca called it "dying limb by limb, the letting out of life drop by drop" (see Seneca, *Letters from a Stoic*). And the Roman jurist Julius Paulus named crucifixion as the worst of all capital punishments, listing it ahead of burning, beheading, or death by wild beasts (see Levy, *Pauli Sententiae*).

Romans usually spared women and Roman citizens from crucifixion, although there were exemptions. But mostly those who were crucified were military enemies, rebellious foreigners, violent criminals, robbers, and especially slaves. In fact, slaves were so routinely crucified that crucifixion became known as the "slaves' punishment" (*servile supplicium*) (see Josephus, *Works*). According to Appian, when the slave rebellion led by Spartacus was crushed, the Roman general Crassus crucified six thousand of the slave prisoners along the Appian Way, the main road leading to Rome (see Appian, *Romaica*). And Josephus tells us that when the Romans began their siege of Jerusalem in 70 CE, the Roman general Titus, who was later to become emperor, would crucify around 500 Jews a day. So many Jews were crucified that "there was not enough room for the crosses nor enough crosses for the victims" (see Josephus, *Works*).

There was much variety in the style of crucifixions, all equally depraved. According to Seneca, "some have their victims' head down on the ground, some impale their private parts, others stretch out their arms on the gibbet" (see Seneca, *Letters from a Stoic*).

The Romans had a special formula for the crucifixion. First, the victim was flogged. The flogging was usually done by two soldiers using a short whip (*flagellum*) made of several pieces of leather thongs. To the thongs were tied small iron balls and sharp pieces of sheep bones. The victim was stripped naked and his hands were tied above his head on a wooden post. The back, buttocks, and legs were scourged until the person collapsed. The blood loss from the flogging would determine how long it would take the crucified person to die on the cross. Many people died from the flogging.

The condemned man was made to carry his own cross to a place of execution outside the city walls. This was not the whole cross, which was too heavy—about three hundred pounds. The part the victim carried on his shoulders was the crossbeam or patibulum, weighing around eighty pounds.

The procession to the execution site included a complete military guard, led by a centurion. The *titulus* or sign telling what the guilty man was accused of was sometimes carried by a soldier or put around the victim's neck. The titulus was later attached to the top of the cross.

There were several places of execution outside Rome. Among the most commonly used was the Campus Equilinus. The Golgotha was used most often outside the gates of Jerusalem. The Golgotha or "place of the skull" was given this name because it was surrounded by hills with caves resembling death heads. At the chosen place of execution, the upright beam of the cross (stipes) was already erected. The patibulum or crossbeam with the man crucified on it would later be hoisted and attached to the stipes.

Roman law stated that upon reaching the place of execution, the victim had to be offered a drink of wine mixed with myrrh *(gall)*. This was a mild narcotic intended to deaden the pain, an ironic show of "mercy" on a cruel and merciless death. The victim was then thrown to the ground on his back, with his arms outstretched along the crossbeam. The arms and hands would then be tied or nailed to the patibulum. Nailing rather than tying was the preferred method used by the Romans. The nails used were made of iron, about seven inches in length with a square head, and they were driven through the wrists.

The victim, now nailed to the patibulum, would be hoisted and attached to the upright beam. There was a small plank of wood *(sedile)* protruding from the stipes, which the crucified man could straddle to absorb some of the weight of the body. At this point the feet were nailed to the stipes, usually one foot on top of the other. Only very rarely, and probably later than the time of Jesus, was an additional block, *suppedaneum*, used to place the feet prior to crucifixion.

There is evidence that in some cases the feet would be nailed through the heel bone on each side of the crossbeam. In 1968, building contractors working on a suburb north of Jerusalem discovered a tomb from the first century CE. In this tomb were found the remains of a man in his twenties, identified as "Jehohanan, son of HGQWL." This man appeared to have been crucified through the side of his heel bones. The iron nail used in the crucifixion was still attached to the bones of the feet. It was about five inches in length. A square piece of olive wood about an inch thick was placed against the side of the heel which was then nailed to the side of the crossbeam. It is clear that the other foot was nailed in the same manner. The remains of this man are kept in the Israel Museum in Jerusalem. Based on this evidence, many scholars believe that Romans did not nail both feet together. They also point out that the thickness of a man's feet would require a nail longer than seven inches to crucify them one on top of the other. This is a matter for controversy but it seems possible for a seven-inch nail to penetrate both feet, especially if the feet were narrow, as they seemed to have been in earlier times when people were smaller than in modern times.

When the nailing of the feet was completed, the titulus was attached to the top of the cross over the victim's head. The length of survival on the cross ranged from three to four hours to three or four days, depending on the physical condition of the victim and the severity of the flogging.

According to medical experts, the most likely cause of death in crucifixion was suffocation. In addition to the excruciating pain caused by the nails driven through bone and sinew, the position of the victim on the cross interfered with normal breathing, especially exhalation. Seneca described this tortured respiration as "drawing the breath of life amid long-drawn agony." There was tremendous strain on the wrists, arms, and shoulders, often resulting in the dislocation of the shoulder and elbow joints. As time passed, the muscles, through loss of blood and lack of oxygen, would undergo severe cramps and spasms. The victim would have to lift his body by pushing on his crucified feet and rotating his elbows in order to be able to exhale. This would cause his back, shredded by the flogging, to scrape against the wood of the cross. He would sustain this agony as long as he was able and then he would slump back on his feet. This alternating motion, up and down on the cross, was the only way the crucified man could remain alive. If he did not push up on the cross he would suffocate and die. This made speech very difficult, if not impossible, as speech takes place during exhalation.

The pitiful attempts of the crucified victims to slide up and down on the cross to be able to exhale prompted the Romans to break their legs so that they could no longer press upwards. This "merciful" action resulted in the quick death of the victims by suffocation. Without the breaking of the legs, a crucified man could hang for days on the cross, the object of jeers and insults; insects crawling on his eyes, mouth, and open wounds; exposed to the elements; unable to eat or drink.

All of these torments were endured by Jesus on the cross. His terrible ordeal began twenty-four hours earlier. On the previous evening he met with his disciples on the upper room of a house let to him by a man of his acquaintance. Once there they observed the feast of Passover. During this last supper Jesus predicted that Judas would betray him and Peter would deny him three times. He also gave bread and wine to his disciples and likened these offerings to his body and blood, thus prophesying his coming ordeal. He then left the upper room and went to the Mount of Olives or Garden of Gethsemane outside the walls of Jerusalem. *Gethsemane* comes from the Hebrew *Gat Shamanim*, meaning "oil press." Today the garden still stands and has many ancient olive trees, some of which may have grown from the roots of the trees that existed in Jesus's time. All trees in and around Jerusalem were razed by the Romans in 70 CE, but olive trees can regenerate from their roots and live for thousands of years.

While in the garden Jesus prayed alone and agonized over what was to come. According to Luke, "his sweat became like great drops of blood falling to the ground" (Luke 22:44). Medical experts say that the sweating of blood is called "hemohidrosis," and it has been seen in patients who have suffered severe stress or shock to their systems (see Allen, *Skin*). But Luke also says that Jesus was alone at this time and that the disciples were all asleep, having failed to keep Jesus company during this time of inner torment. How, then, did he know that Jesus sweated blood? Only Jesus himself could have told him this. But when did Jesus make this revelation to Luke, since Jesus was taken prisoner shortly afterward and did not speak again to his disciples?

While Jesus was still at Gethsemane he was betrayed by Judas and arrested by the Jews. All his disciples fled and abandoned him. He was first brought to Annas, the father-in-law of the high priest Caiaphas, for a preliminary examination. Annas sent him to Caiaphas, and a general council was summoned to take action on the teachings of Jesus. When Caiaphas asked Jesus if he was indeed the Messiah (Christ), the son of God, Jesus answered, "I am." Caiaphas considered this a blasphemy deserving the penalty of death. The sentence was ratified at a formal meeting of the Sanhedrin, the Supreme National Tribunal of the Jews, which consisted of seventy-one members. But since Caiaphas did not have the authority to carry out the sentence, he sent Jesus to Pontius Pilate, the Roman military governor or procurator of Judea.

When Jesus was brought to Pilate, the charges against him were changed. Instead of blasphemy, he was charged by the Sanhedrin as pretending to be a king who did not advocate the paying of taxes to the Romans. Before pronouncing sentence, Pilate asked Jesus if he was the King of the Jews. Jesus answered, "It is as you say" (Matthew 27:11). In spite of the charges, Pilate did not find any fault with Jesus and sent him to Herod, the King of the Jews. Jesus was silent before Herod and the king sent him back to Pilate.

The gospels tell us that Pilate was unconvinced of Jesus's guilt and called the chief priests and the people and told them that as he found no guilt in Jesus he was only going to chastise him and then release him. This was part of a custom where a condemned man would be released at the time of the Passover feast. The chief priests and the crowd rejected Pilate's suggestion and demanded that Jesus be crucified and another prisoner, called Barrabas, be released instead. Three times Pilate asked the crowd to reconsider Jesus's fate, but in the end they prevailed and Pilate was forced to crucify Jesus.

It was at this time that Jesus underwent the flogging that preceded each Roman crucifixion. The number of strikes is not recorded in the gospels. The number of blows in Jewish law was set in Deuteronomy 25:3 at forty, but later reduced to thirty-nine to prevent excessive blows by a counting error. Roman law did not put any limits on the number of blows given during scourging. It may have been thirty-nine, or it may have been more or less.

After the flogging, the Roman soldiers put a scarlet robe around Jesus's shoulders, probably the cloak of an army officer. They twisted together a crown of thorns and placed it on his head. They put a staff in his right hand and knelt mockingly in front of him and hailed him as King of the Jews. Unlike the traditional crown of thorns depicted in many paintings, the actual crown may have covered the entire scalp. The thorns may have been one to two inches long. According to the gospels, the Roman soldiers continued to beat Jesus on the head. These blows would have driven the thorns deeper into the forehead and scalp, causing painful abrasions and bleeding.

We must remember that Jesus had not slept the previous night, which he spent in a lonely vigil at Gethsemane. Thus he must have been exhausted and weakened by the various trials and the flogging and the head beatings. In these conditions, he was forced to carry the patibulum across his shoulders and walk to the Golgotha, the designated place of his crucifixion.

The distance he walked has been estimated at about 650 yards. This path, now known as the Via Dolorosa, led through a narrow street of stone, probably surrounded by markets at the time. On the way, he fell three times under the heavy weight, prompting the Roman soldiers to ask a bystander called Simon of Cyrene (currently North Africa) to help Jesus carry the crossbeam.

Upon arrival at the Golgotha, Jesus was offered the drink of wine and myrrh that was meant to lessen the pain of crucifixion, but he refused it. He was then crucified to the crossbeam and hoisted to the stipes, where the crossbeam was attached. Above his head, the Romans placed the titulus consisting of four Latin letters: INRI, meaning Iesus Nazarenus Rex Iudaerum, Jesus of Nazareth, King of the Jews. Earlier the chief priests argued the use of these letters, asking Pilate to change the titulus to read that Jesus claimed he was King of the Jews. But Pilate said, "What I have written, I have written." Of his disciples, only John was present at the crucifixion. Many women who had followed him were there, among them his mother Mary, Salome, and Mary Magdalene.

The time of the crucifixion, according to Mark, was three in the afternoon. On the ninth hour the same evangelist says that Jesus died on the cross. This means that Jesus stayed on the cross for six hours. His legs, contrary to Roman custom, were not broken. According to John, one of the soldiers, to ensure Jesus was dead, pierced his side with his spear. A mixture of blood and water ensued from the wound.

A follower of Jesus, Joseph of Arimathea, a wealthy Jew who was probably a member of the Sanhedrin, went to Pilate after Jesus's death to claim his body. Pilate expressed surprise that Jesus was already dead but released his body in the care of Arimathea, who brought Jesus's body down from the cross, wrapped it in fine linen, and placed it in a new tomb.

The Romans used two crosses during crucifixions, the long and the short cross. This latter was about seven feet tall. Most scholars believe that the cross used in Jesus's crucifixion was the short version. They base this view on the fact that when Jesus said he was thirsty, one of the soldiers offered him a drink of wine vinegar from a sponge placed on the stalk of a hyssop plant. This stalk is approximately twenty inches long, strongly supporting the belief that Jesus was crucified on the short cross. The fact that Jesus's side was pierced by a lance also indicates the cross must have been the short version.

So far we have been looking at Jesus's crucifixion from the gospels' point of view. Let us now look at what various experts say on the subject. On March 21, 1986, the Journal of the American Medical Association published an article titled "On the Physical Death of Jesus Christ." The article was authored by Dr. William D. Edwards, a pathologist from the Mayo Clinic; Floyd Z. Hosmer, an expert in Medical Graphics from the same institution; and Wesley J. Gabel, a pastor from the West Bethel United Methodist Church in Minnesota. The article gives detailed information on Jesus's crucifixion and the traumas he suffered during this ordeal. The medical data is impressive in its wealth of detail, and the conclusion of the writers was that Jesus died before the wound to his side was inflicted and that the wound itself, if thrust on the right side, would have ensured his death by piercing the right lung and the heart. In their opinion, the assumption that Jesus did not die on the cross is at odds with modern medical knowledge. This opinion rests on the idea that Jesus was pierced on the right side and that the length of the spear was long enough to inflict a severe wound. If the spear entered through the right side, a large flow of blood would be more likely with the perforation of the thin-walled right ventricle of the heart. On the other hand, if it entered through the left, the thick-walled and contracted left ventricle would have been difficult to pierce. The writers assume in the light of artistic depictions of the crucifixion that the spear entered through the right, but in reality we do not know for sure. The only gospel that mentions this wound is that of John and the evangelist never says which side of Jesus was pierced. The article also leaves unanswered the question that if the wound was indeed inflicted, it may not have been a deep thrust of the spear but a short jab.

On the opposite side of the argument there is a learned and well-documented article by Dr. Joe Zia, the curator of archeology/anthropology for the Israel Antiquities Authority from 1972 to 1997. Dr. Zia is now retired and lectures throughout the world.

In Dr. Zia's view, while many researchers believe that Jesus's death was the result of a ruptured heart because of the story in John 19:34 of blood and water flowing from Jesus' pierced side, many pathologists, such as Frederick T. Zugibe (*The Cross and the Shroud*, 1984), have ruled this out as medically untenable. Other scholars have regarded asphyxiation as the cause of death, but according to Dr. Zia the latest research findings have shown the issue to be more complicated, depending upon the manner in which the victim was crucified. In a series of experiments carried out by Dr. Zugibe with the help of college students who volunteered to be tied to crosses, if the students were suspended from crosses with their arms outstretched in the traditional manner depicted in Christian art, they experienced no problem breathing. This indicates that death on the cross as the result of suffocation cannot happen if arms are outstretched, as in the case of Jesus. Moreover, if the upright beam has a sedile or small seat, which the victim can straddle for support of the body, death can be prolonged by days. According to Josephus (*Jewish Antiquities*), three of his friends were crucified by the Romans. Upon intervention by Josephus to Titus, they were removed from their crosses and with medical care one of them survived.

Did Jesus survive the crucifixion? The controversy is growing, with an increasing number of experts questioning Jesus's short time on the cross, the fact that his legs were not broken, and that Pilate himself expressed surprise at his quick death.

It is certain that Jesus must have been thoroughly exhausted by his long appearances before Annas, the Sanhedrin, Herod, and Pilate. The flogging and beatings by the Roman soldiers must have further weakened his condition, exemplified by the fact that he needed help to carry the patibulum. But all crucifixion victims endured similar punishments and often worse, and some lasted days on the cross. Furthermore, Jesus was a young carpenter of thirty-two or thirty-three years of age in excellent physical health. We know this because in the course of his ministry he had to walk on foot throughout Judea and its environs. The gospels indicate that he ate and drank well and was of a robust disposition (Luke 7:34). His good health would have been of great help in en-during the torments of the crucifixion.

We are told by the gospels that Jesus refused the mild narcotic of-fered by Roman soldiers to crucifixion victims. This refusal ensured his alertness during the crucifixion and his ability to remain alive as long as possible. We know that he spoke seven times from the cross, not an easy task if he had been struggling to exhale. But if we take into con-sideration Dr. Zugibe's experiment, maybe breathing was not as diffi-cult during crucifixion as it was at first believed.

We know there were varied ways of crucifixion. Some of them were more extreme than others. There is no way to know for sure if Jesus's arms and hands were only tied to the cross or maybe tied and nailed. We do know that the two thieves who were executed next to him were not nailed but tied to their crosses (Luke 25:39). Luke is the only evan-gelist who uses the word "hanged" in the gospels, just like John is the only one who says that blood and water issued from Jesus's pierced side. These discrepancies between the evangelists only serve to add fuel to the controversy surrounding Jesus's crucifixion.

One thing all the four gospels agree on is that Jesus died on the cross. The synoptics say that Jesus commended his soul to God and then his head fell upon his chest and he breathed his last. But was he really dead? Mark, Luke, and Matthew were not present at the crucifix-ion and, in any case, their gospels were written many years later by writers using their names. They did not witness Jesus's death on the cross. John alone was present at this event and it is almost certain he wrote the gospel that bears his name. Therefore it is John's gospel that we should pay close attention to. What John says on the death of Jesus was that after drinking the wine vinegar offered to him, Jesus ex-claimed, "It is finished. And bowing his head, he gave up his spirit." (John 19:30). From his place at the foot of the cross, at least seven feet away, John could not tell if Jesus had indeed died or fainted.

It is consistent with present medical research that a person who has suffered severe trauma to his body and his mind may enter into a

coma, not unlike death. As John, who was an actual witness to the crucifixion, says that Jesus's side was pierced, we must take his assertion
seriously. But then John says something that has caused much specula-
tion in medical circles. He says that blood and then water issued from
the wound. Some experts consider this medically impossible and there
is no way to get around that fact except by assuming that John may
have been confused and water flowed before blood.

After Joseph of Arimathea laid Jesus's body on the new tomb, a man
called Nicodemus, another follower of Jesus, brought about a hundred
pounds of myrrh and aloes to the tomb. Then between Nicodemus
and Joseph of Arimathea they bound the body of Jesus in strips of
linen with the spices in the prescribed Jewish form of burial of the day.
John tells us this (John 19:39–40). But two days later, when Mary Magdalene went to the tomb, she found it open and empty. She immediately went to find Peter and John, and told them what she had seen.
Upon arriving at the tomb, the disciples found the linen cloths and the
handkerchief that had been tied around Jesus's head folded in a place
by itself. Later on, the same day, Mary Magdalene saw Jesus standing
near the tomb, but she did not recognize him even though he spoke to
her and she answered him. Only when he called her by her name did
she realize who he was (John 20:15–16). Why didn't Mary Magdalene
recognize Jesus? Was it really Jesus whom she saw? If he was, he must
have been vastly altered in his physical appearance for her to fail to recognize him. A man who had recently undergone the torments of a crucifixion and who was beaten on the head would certainly show some
disfigurement.

Jesus appeared to his disciples several times after this and even ate
with them, according to the gospels. The question is was he a spirit or
a living man? Luke is the only gospel that speaks of Jesus's physical ascension to heaven. Today, most theological scholars consider this vision
symbolic, instead of an actual event.

There are several unsubstantiated reports that place Jesus in India or
Syria after the crucifixion. There is even an account where Jesus trav-

eled with Mary through Persia, where he became known as Yuz Asaf, "leader of the healed." The apocryphal Acts of Thomas describe the stay of Jesus and Thomas in Taxila (now in Pakistan). East of Taxila there is a small town called Murree, near the modern border with Kashmir. In Murree there is a grave which has been honored and maintained since time immemorial called *Mai Mari da Asthan*, the "final resting place of Mother Mary." Muslims honor the grave because Mary was Jesus's mother and Jesus (Issa or Isa) is considered one of the most important prophets of Islam. The Koran states that Jesus was saved from dying on the cross, which is considered an accursed death (Deuteronomy 21:23) and unworthy of him.

After this Jesus is said to have traveled to Kashmir and from there to India. There is a grave in the middle of a small town called Srinagar that many people believe to be Jesus's grave. The building erected around the gravesite is called Rozabal, the "tomb of a prophet." Within the inner burial chamber there are two gravestones, the larger for Yuz Asaf (Jesus) and the smaller for an Islamic saint of the sixteenth century.

The Indian Mogul emperor Akbar, who lived in the sixteenth century, selected one saying of Jesus to inscribe on the wall of his Victory Gate (see *Cambridge History of India*). This saying, unknown to the West, was found on a piece of wall among the ruins of a city built by Akbar. It says:

> Said Jesus, on whom be peace! The world is a bridge, pass over it but build no house there. He who hopes for an hour, hopes for eternity; the world is but an hour, spend it in devotion; the rest is worth nothing.

Jesus may or may not have traveled to India after the crucifixion, but even some of the church's early fathers believed he survived the ordeal. The second century church father Irenaeus wrote a famous book called *Against Heresies*. In this book he claimed Jesus lived to be an old man and remained in Asia with his disciple John and others, up to the times of the Emperor Trajan, before finally dying. As Trajan began his reign in 98 CE, this would mean that Jesus lived well past 100 years of age.

The case for Jesus' survival after the crucifixion is vital to his own claim that he was the Messiah. It was impossible for the Messiah to have died on the cross. The book of Deuteronomy (21:22) is clear on death by hanging on a tree, and the cross is made from a tree:

> If a man has committed a sin worthy of death, and he is put to death, and you hang him on a tree, his body shall not remain overnight on the tree, but you shall surely bury him that day, so that you do not defile the land which the Lord your God is giving you as an inheritance; for he who is hanged is accursed of God.

The Christian claim that Jesus died on the tree of the cross is one of the most powerful reasons why orthodox Jews do not accept him as the Messiah. Paul's flaunting of Jewish traditional observances added to this rejection. But the Messiah is a Jewish concept. A Messiah cannot be a Hindu, a Christian, a Muslim, or a member of any other religion but Judaism. And he must adhere to the tenets of the messianic tradition and uphold the Torah—the Mosaic Law—to be accepted as a true Messiah.

Furthermore, as we saw in an earlier chapter, the Messiah must have a son who carries on his father's work.

If Jesus died on the cross, he could not have been the Messiah, and ultimately, that was his most important claim. By virtue of its insistence on Jesus's death on the cross and his celibacy, Christianity is denying Jesus's own words.

It is significant that the gospel of Mark, considered by scholars to have been the first gospel, upon which both Matthew and Luke were based, does not mention Jesus's resurrection from the dead. According to Mark, Jesus did not appear to Mary Magdalene or to the disciples after the crucifixion. All this gospel says is that when Mary Magdalene, Mary the mother of James, and Salome came to the tomb after the end of the Sabbath, they found it open and empty. Inside the tomb they found a young man dressed in a white robe who told them Jesus was not there but that he would appear to his disciples later, as he had told them he would. The women flew away in terror. That is the end of the gospel (Mark 16:8). The other gospel writers added to Mark's original story, embellishing it with accounts of Jesus's resurrection and his appearance to Mary Magdalene and the disciples. There are several alternate endings to Mark's gospel but biblical scholars agree that it undoubtedly ended at 16:8.

It is believed by most biblical scholars that Mark's gospel was probably written in the wake of Nero's persecution of Christians in 64 CE. This date is consistent with Mark's emphasis on the tribulations of Jesus and his followers (Mark 4–17; 10:30; 13–9). Mark and Luke are believed to have been written toward the end of the first century CE.

Ultimately, Jesus's death on the cross solves nothing. It is not his death that matters, but his life. It is his personal integrity, his courage, and the powerful message of his teachings that have transformed the world. Jesus's death on the cross would not have redeemed for long the sins of the world, for the world would continue to sin long after his proclaimed and vilified "death."

The word Christ is derived from the Greek Christos, meaning the "anointed one," the Messiah, in Hebrew Mashiakh. Jesus Christ means, literally, Jesus the Messiah.

Jesus as the Messiah is a symbol of hope. He is a divine messenger upon whose transcendental shoulders rests the destiny of a suffering humanity. He is the Sun of Tiphareth, the light of the world. Therefore, through kabbalistic reasoning we must believe that Jesus did not die on the cross. He survived the crucifixion and lived for many years, carrying his message of brotherly love through the many lands of his forced exile. His suffering on the cross was part of his chosen mission. His survival of his ordeal was proof of his own healing powers. If he could heal others, he could surely heal himself.

He said once, "I am the way, the truth, and the life. No one comes to the Father except through me." Tiphareth, which represents Jesus, is the way to Kether and to Eheieh, God before manifestation.

9

JESUS ON THE TREE

I am the way, the truth, and the life.
No one comes to the Father
except through me.

—JESUS (JOHN 14:6)

The cross has always been identified as a tree. In Acts 12:29, Luke says, "they took him down from the tree and laid him in a tomb." Referring to Jesus's death on the cross, Peter says, "who himself bore our sins in his own body on the tree"(1 Peter 2:24).

The Tree of Life has been connected with Jesus by many of the early Christian writers. It is interesting in this context that the first mention of the Tree of Life is in the first book of the Old Testament (Genesis) and the last reference to the tree is in the last book of the New (Revelation). In Revelation 2:7, John speaks of "the Tree of Life in the midst of the Paradise of God." In this versicle, Jesus, who is depicted by John as holding seven stars in his right hand and walking among seven golden lamps, is addressing the church at Ephesus and promises them that he will give them permission to eat from the Tree of Life if they resist evil.

Two of the images associated with the sixth Sephira, Tiphareth, are those of a majestic king and a sacrificed god. Both images are related to Jesus in the Christian Kabbalah. The planet associated with Tiphareth is the Sun, also a symbol of Jesus, who said, "I am the light of the world."

The seven stars that Jesus held in his hand in Revelation and the seven golden lamps among which he walked were symbols of the seven churches, but they are also symbols of the seven lower Sephiroth of the Tree of Life.

The Sun of Tiphareth illuminates the seven Sephiroth from its position on the center of the tree. Malkuth receives only the reflected light of Tiphareth through Yesod (the Moon), which stands between them.

The name of Jesus in Hebrew is Yeshua. It is made of four letters: Yod, Shin, Vau, Ayin. As we saw in chapter 6, Yod symbolizes a hand; it is steady-state continuity, cause, perfection, power, and generation. Shin symbolizes a tooth; it is the spirit of God, transformation, renewal. Vau symbolizes a nail; it is the archetype of fertilizing substances, union, dependency, relationships. Ayin symbolizes an eye; it is the illuminating principle behind impregnation, understanding, source, prevention.

Through their kabbalistic symbolism, the letters of Yeshua signify a continuous cause and generating power that, through the spirit of God, transforms and renews. It is the union that makes creation possible through the fertilization of all species, and it does so through union, understanding, and the prevention of negative influences. It is the source of positive cosmic action. Furthermore, the symbols of the letters—a hand, a tooth, a nail, and an eye—add significantly to the meaning of Yeshua. The hand and the nail can be understood immediately as the symbols of crucifixion. The tooth is used to masticate, an important tool in food absorption, essential for the regeneration and renewal of body tissues and thus of life. The eye represents vigilance and awareness, also essential for the prevention of any danger, physical or spiritual.

Yeshua's name reveals his spiritual mission, and that it would be accomplished through the ultimate sacrifice of the crucifixion.

The book of Genesis tells us that when the patriarch Abram was ninety-nine years old, the Lord appeared to Abram and said, "I am Almighty God; walk before Me and be blameless. And I will make my covenant between Me and you, and will multiply you exceedingly. No longer shall your name be called Abram, but your name shall be Abraham." The Lord also instructed Abraham to change the name of his wife Sarai to Sarah. To ratify this covenant, Abraham, his sons, and all the males of his house had to undergo circumcision, the sign of the covenant between Abraham and God.

By adding the letter H to Abram's and Sarai's names, what God did was give them one of the *He*'s from the Tetragrammaton, Yod, He, Vau, He. By doing this, he ratified the covenant and made Abraham and Sarah participants in a cosmic alliance that would last through many generations.

All the Hebrew patriarchs had this H in their names: Isaac (Itshak), Moses (Moshe), and Solomon (Shlomo). God changed Jacob's name to Israel (Ishroel) when he renewed Abraham's covenant with Jacob, thus giving him the He in the new name. Only David did not receive the holy letter because he broke his covenant with God through the murder of Uriah, Bathsheba's husband.

By adding He to Yeshua we get Yeheshua, Jesus's true name. It means "Jehovah is deliverance." And if we add the letter Shin from Yeshua's name to Yod He Vau He, we also get Yeheshua. Shin also symbolizes the spark of light who is God, identified with the Holy Spirit or Ruach Elohim. The transference of both the He and the Shin speaks of a mutual covenant between God and Jesus.

The cross is identified with the four cardinal points, the four elements, and the four letters of the Tetragrammaton (see Figure 8). The top part of the cross and its two horizontal extensions symbolize the first three spheres of the Tree of Life. The last seven spheres are symbolized by the rest of the upright beam. As the cross represents the Tetragrammaton, Jesus accomplishes the mission hidden in his name by being crucified to the divine name, one of whose letters (Vau) means nail. Yod signifies hand (extremity, and also foot by association). The hands and the feet of Jesus are nailed to the cross, the Tetragrammaton.

The letter He signifies window, an opening, through which may enter the light of the Sun, air, and life; it also means love. The two *He*'s in Yod He Vau He and in Yeheshua represent a duality of love, God's

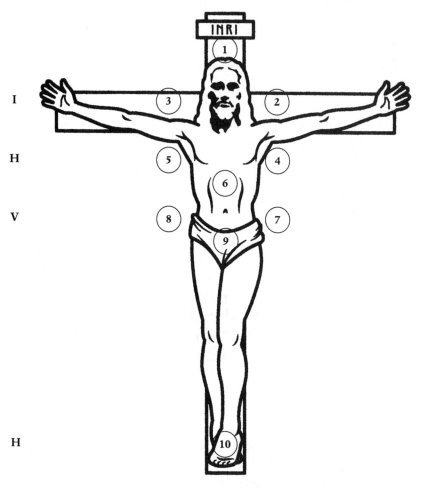

I

H

V

H

Figure 8: The Ten Sephiroth and the Crucified Christ.

divine love and Jesus's human love. As we saw, Yeheshua means "Jehovah is deliverance," salvation. Jesus represents the salvation of the world through the power of the divine name. His opened arms on the cross are a symbol of his great love for humanity.

The seven lower Sephiroth, represented by the lower part of the upright beam of the cross, have their center in Tiphareth, the sixth Sephira and the sphere of the Sun. When Jesus said, "I am the light of the world. I am the Way. No one comes to the Father except through me," he was identifying himself with Tiphareth, the Sun, the light of the world. As Tiphareth is the sphere on the Middle Pillar that leads straight to Kether, it is indeed the way to God, the Creator, the Father.

Between Tiphareth and Kether we find the hidden sphere, Daath. This is not a true Sephira. It is a gate, the gap created by the fall, which must be bridged to attain the qualities of the first three Sephiroth and reach God. That is the reason why God's name in Tiphareth is Jehovah elo ve Daath, where IHVH opens the gate of Daath to lead to AHIH, the divine name in Kether. As Daath is placed on the throat, it gives rise to the powers of speech, to communication. It was through communication, through his oral teachings, that Jesus illuminated the world.

As we have seen, the four letters in the titulus over Jesus's head were INRI. These letters meant *Iesus Nazarenus Rex Iudaerum*, Jesus King of the Jews. When these letters are transliterated into Hebrew they become Yod Nun Resh Yod. We have seen the symbolism of Yod before as both a hand, continuity, power and cause. Nun's symbol is a fish; it also means individual existence, expansion, increase. Resh symbolizes the head; its meaning is a higher state of Beth, universal container. It is also associated with intelligence, perspicacity, and ideas.

The double Yod in INRI again points to Jesus's crucified hands. Nun and Resh speak of an individual existence characterized by great intelligence and lofty ideas. While Resh symbolizes the head, Nun represents a fish. This was the earliest symbol of Christianity. In Roman times, Christians used the symbol of a fish to identify each other.

INRI is also associated with the four letters of the Tetragrammaton and the four points of the cross, the four elements, the four cardinal points, and the four dimensions. It also falls under the aegis of the Sephiroth of the Tree of Life as follows:

Kether

I

Binah   Chokmah

Geburah   Chesed

N

Tiphareth

Hod   Netzach

R

Yesod

I

Malkuth

The first I or Yod is associated with the first triad of the Tree of Life, comprising Kether, Chokmah, and Binah. It symbolizes the element of air, the most subtle of the divine emanations. It represents the astrological triplicity of the air signs Gemini, Libra, and Aquarius.

The N is associated with the second triad, composed of Chesed, Geburah, and Tiphareth. It symbolizes the element of fire. It represents the astrological triplicity of the fire signs Aries, Leo, and Sagittarius. All these signs are ruled by planets associated with fire: Mars, the Sun, and Jupiter.

The R is associated with the third triad, composed of Netzach, Hod, and Yesod. It symbolizes the element of water. It represents the astrological triplicity of the water signs Cancer, Scorpio, and Pisces.

The last I is associated with the lone Sephira, Malkuth, and symbolizes the element of earth.

On the cross, Jesus's head lies below the sphere of Kether, between Chokmah and Binah (see Figure 8). It is represented by the first Yod of both IHVH and INRI. This Yod (hand) is a symbol of the crucifixion.

You will note that the letter associated with Path 32, leading from Malkuth (the Earth) to Yesod (the Moon), is Tau. This is the first Path that must be traversed on the ascent on the tree. Tau is a cross. It was the shape of the cross most commonly used by the Romans during crucifixions. It may have been used to crucify Jesus. Tau is the last letter of the Hebrew alphabet. It means death, but also return, plenitude. It is redemption. Tau is the Path that leads to the illumination of Yesod (the Moon). If we follow the Path of the Arrow through the Middle Pillar, Tau (the cross) will lead us through Yesod to Tiphareth (the Sun) and hence to Kether.

Path 25, represented by the letter Samekh, symbolizes support, source, knowledge. It connects the sphere of Yesod to Tiphareth. It means that the source of knowledge is the light of God.

Path 13, represented by the letter Gimel, symbolizes realization, splendor. It connects Tiphareth to Kether. It means the realization and splendor of union with God.

We can see that the colors ascribed to the spheres of the Tree of Life in the Briatic scale are the colors of the solar spectrum.

Kether is white light, light before differentiation.

Chokmah is a pearly grey, an iridescent greyish white, where the light is beginning to differentiate.

Binah is black, the absorption of the light, emanated by Kether through Chokmah; it is the cosmos.

Chesed is blue, the color of the sky as the cosmos brightens with the light emanated from Binah.

Geburah is red, the color of blood, of life.

Tiphareth is yellow, the color of sunlight, the nourishment of the world.

Netzach is green, the color of the plants, the givers of oxygen and the breath of life.

Hod is orange, the energy of mind.

Malkuth has four colors: russet, citrine, olive, and black. These are the colors of the Earth and a mixture of the colors of the other spheres.

You will note that the mixture of yellow and blue (Tiphareth and Chesed) gives us green, the color of Netzach, directly below Chesed. The mixture of yellow and red (Tiphareth and Geburah) gives us orange, the color of Hod, directly under Geburah. We see in the solar spectrum that yellow is in the center and that orange is on its right side and green on its left, the result of the mixture of yellow with red and blue, respectively. At the opposite sides of the spectrum are red and violet. This last color is a mixture of red and blue, indicating that the spectrum doubles upon itself to make a circle, where red and blue meet to make violet. This circle and the color violet are identified with Yesod and the Moon.

In the Tree of Life, the mixture of the blue of Chesed and the red of Geburah produce the color violet of Yesod, the Moon. The union of Chesed and Geburah also create the Mogen David (the Star of David, a symbol of Judaism and the Messiah).

The Star of David is made of two interlaced triangles. The upper triangle, pointing upward, represents fire; the lower, pointing downward, represents water. The union of these two essentially opposite elements symbolizes David's great work in uniting the dissident twelve tribes of Israel. Fire is associated with the color red, and water with blue. As these two colors unite to form violet, we find ourselves in the sphere of Yesod, the Moon. The importance of the Moon in Judaism is very marked. The Jewish calendar is lunar. And one of the great *mitzvah* or ordinances of the Jewish religion is the chanting of the Hallel (*Hallel-u-Jah*, praises to God) on the day of the New Moon. The Hallel is composed of several of David's psalms, notably Psalm 81, which calls for the sounding of the ram horn *(shofar)* at the New Moon.

David was Israel's Messiah prior to Jesus and we have seen how Jesus quoted David's Psalm 22 from the cross to reiterate his claim as David's reincarnation as the true Messiah.

Yesod, the Moon, is therefore our connection with the light of Tiphareth. That is why the Hallel is chanted on the New Moon and the Moon is connected to all major religious holidays in Judaism.

One of the most important parts of the observance of the day of the Sabbath, when the Shekinah unites with her holy bridegroom, is the offering of bread and wine.

The first ritual offering of bread and wine was conducted by the high priest Melchizedek (Gen. 14:18). Melchizedek was King of Salem (righteousness and peace) and a priest of God. He brought out bread and wine, blessed them, and blessed Abram and God, giving a tithe (a tenth part) of the offering to Abram. After this, God made his covenant with the patriarch, changing his name to Abraham. A tithe is a reference to the ten Sephiroth of the Tree of Life. Melchizedek divided the offering in ten parts and gave one to Abram, clearly denoting Malkuth, the beginning of the road to God.

Melchizedek was the first and greatest of all priests sacred to God. He was identified with the Elohim. He is a divine and eternal priest. David's Psalm 110 is known as an Announcement of the Messiah's Reign. In this psalm, God makes David a priest forever "according to the order of Melchizedek" (Psalm 110:4). The Epistle to the Hebrews also speaks of Jesus as a "high priest forever according to the order of Melchizedek" (Heb. 6:20). This again underlines the bond between David and Jesus.

During the Last Supper, Jesus blessed bread and wine, as Melchizedek had done, and gave them to his disciples. He did this to establish a new covenant with them and with the world. When he broke the bread, blessed it, and gave it to the disciples, he said, "Take, eat; this is my body." He then blessed the wine and gave it to them to drink and said, "This is my blood, of the new covenant, which is shed for many" (Mark 14:22, 24). As Melchizedek had given bread and wine to Abram before his covenant with God, so did Jesus, as a "high priest forever according to the order of Melchizedek," give bread and wine to his disciples to establish a new covenant. This covenant was ratified through the shedding of his blood during the crucifixion. The blood is part of the covenant. In God's covenant with Abram, the blood shed was that of circumcision.

Jesus's mission as the Messiah is an intrinsic part of him and his work. His undeniable presence on the Tree of Life is an avowal of his identity as the Messiah. But he could not be the Messiah if he died on the cross. He could not be the Messiah if he was celibate. And he could not be the Messiah if he was born through a virgin birth because that would deny him the genealogy to David, which could only be received through his father Joseph's line.

IO

THE TEACHER

Jesus went throughout Galilee,
teaching in their synagogues and
proclaiming the good news
of the kingdom . . .

—MATT. 4-23

Jesus began his ministry at the age of thirty (Luke 3:23). The synoptic gospels, Matthew, Mark, and Luke, say that this happened after the imprisonment of John the Baptist. John dates the event after Jesus chose his first disciples. The synoptics tell us Jesus's ministry lasted for approximately one year, while John says it lasted for nearly three years. It is John's dating that gives us Jesus's most commonly accepted age—thirty-three—at the time of the crucifixion.

After his baptism by John the Baptist, Jesus retired to the wilderness for forty days, a period during which he meditated and fasted and was tempted by the devil. Some biblical scholars consider these forty days as a ritual of preparation for his future ministry.

At the end of this self-imposed spiritual retreat, Jesus returned to Galilee. He began to teach in the synagogues and was praised by everyone. He then visited his home in Nazareth. He went to the synagogue on the Sabbath day, as was his custom, and stood up to read from the scriptures. He was given the scroll of the prophet Isaiah. Jesus unrolled the scroll and found the passage where it is written:

> The Spirit of the Lord is upon me, because he has anointed me to bring good news to the poor. He has sent me to proclaim release to the captives and recovery of sight to the blind, to let the oppressed go free, to proclaim the year of the Lord's favor.

Jesus then rolled up the scroll, gave it back to the attendant, and sat down. All the eyes of the people in the synagogue were fixed on him, as he was expected to comment on the passage. He began by saying, "Today this scripture has been fulfilled in your hearing." Then he proceeded to compare his work with the works of the prophets Elijah and Elisha, and told them that no prophet would be accepted in his own hometown. These remarks so enraged the members of the synagogue that they drove Jesus out of town and nearly threw him off a cliff. But Jesus passed through their midst, as if unseen, and left Nazareth (Luke 4:14–29).

After his rejection in Nazareth, Jesus went on to Capernaum and began healing people and teaching in the synagogues. Everywhere he went he was accepted. It was shortly after this that he chose his first disciples, Simon Peter, John, and James. The rest of the disciples were chosen much later.

The core of Jesus's teachings was given by him to his disciples and a large crowd on the Sermon on the Mount (Matt. 5:1–7:27). Luke calls the same event the Sermon on the Plain (Luke 6:17) but does not expand on Jesus's teachings as lengthily as Matthew. Both Luke and Matthew cite the Beatitudes, where Jesus blesses the poor, the meek, the peacemakers, and others who will receive mercy and gain the kingdom of heaven. This is the beginning of this famous sermon. Matthew then presents us with Jesus's main body of teachings. It is during this sermon that Jesus says he did not come to abolish the law or the prophets but to fulfill them. He then proceeds to teach about adultery, improper judgment, the loving of enemies, praying in the privacy of one's room, and false prophets. He also teaches the listening crowd the proper way to pray the Paternoster.

Throughout the teachings in the sermon and in other of Jesus's teachings, we find definite kabbalistic links. In the sermon he entreats his listeners not to concern themselves with material needs. "Consider the lilies of the field, how they grow; they neither toil nor spin; yet I tell you, even Solomon in all his glory was not clothed like one of these. Therefore do not worry, saying, What will we eat? What will we drink? What will we wear? But strive first for the kingdom of God and these things will be given to you as well." The kingdom of God is Malkuth, and proper meditation on this sphere will accomplish whatever a person may desire.

Earlier in the sermon Jesus says, "If anyone strikes you on the right cheek, turn the other also; and if anyone wants your coat, give him your cloak also; and if anyone forces you to go one mile, go also the second mile." Many people believe that this is a teaching of humility. It is not. It refers to what is known as "the Law of Three." This is a cosmic law based on the three triads of the Tree of Life. This law says that whoever hurts you will receive punishment three times stronger than what he meted you. Whoever helps you will receive thrice the reward for his aid. Likewise, if you hurt or help someone, you will also receive punishment or reward in a threefold measure. Therefore, according to this teaching of Jesus, it is not necessary to avenge yourself on an attacker. If he strikes you only once on the right cheek, he will receive a threefold punishment for his deed. But if you offer the other cheek, the punishment is further multiplied by three, making it six times over what you received. That is punishment indeed and you do not have to break God's law, which says that vengeance is the Lord's.

Jesus was also referring to the Law of Three when he instructed his listeners on how to give alms: "Whenever you give alms, do not sound a trumpet before you, as the hypocrites do in the synagogues and in the streets, so they may be praised by others. Truly I tell you, they have received their reward. But when you give alms, do not let your left hand know what your right hand is doing, so that your alms may be done in secret: and your Father who sees in secret will reward you." The secrecy is of paramount importance in all kabbalistic work. It is in fact one of the laws of the adept: "Be silent." Without secrecy, the cosmic energy that is concentrated during a meditative or magical act is dispersed. That is why Jesus said that giving alms publicly is its own reward. The Law of Three no longer applies.

Jesus said in the same sermon, "Ask and it will be given you; search and you will find; knock, and the door will be opened to you." He was referring to the search for wisdom (Chokmah) through which all things are possible.

Mark tells us that before the death of John the Baptist, Jesus called his twelve disciples and began to send them out two by two, giving them authority over unclean spirits (Mark 6:7). He ordered them to take nothing for their journey except a staff. They were to take no bread, no money in their belts, but to wear sandals and only one tunic. He said to them, "Whenever you enter a house, stay there until you leave the place. If any place will not welcome you and they refuse to hear you, as you leave, shake off the dust of your sandals as a testimony against them" (Mark 6:8). Matthew adds to this "testimony": "Truly I tell you, it will be more tolerable for the land of Sodom and Gomorrah on the day of judgment than for that town."

One of my friends, who is a biblical scholar and a firm believer in the power of Jesus's teachings, had the opportunity to test this particular teaching. When she was still a student at Columbia's Law School, she was living with her husband, also a student, in New York City. Like most students, their funds were very limited and their bills were often paid late. One day they received a notification from Con Edison, the provider of electricity for the city of New York, telling them that their electricity was about to be turned off for nonpayment of their last bill. They quickly borrowed money from several friends for the amount of the bill and my friend went immediately to Con Edison's offices to make the payment. But when she arrived there, she was told that because of her late payment record, she had to give the company a deposit of $300. Without that deposit, her electricity would be turned off the next day. All her pleas for a few days' extension fell on deaf ears. The manager who had been summoned to hear her case refused to grant the extension. My friend left Con Edison's offices filled with humiliation and dismay. She felt that the company's representative had treated her with the most appalling lack of understanding and compassion. All she had asked for was a few days' extension so that she could ask her parents to loan her the deposit money. To deny this simple request, in her view, was unconscionable. As she stepped outside the company's door, she remembered Jesus's teaching to his disciples about shaking the dust off their shoes on the doorstep of whoever refused to listen to their words. Still filled with indignation at the manager's callousness, she stamped her feet several times at Con Edison's door and asked for divine justice. That evening as she and her husband watched the news on television, she heard how one of Con Edison's plants had had an inexplicable break in their circuitry. As a result, many of their computers crashed, erasing the accounts of thousands of their customers. Her account was among those erased. Naturally, she did not have to pay the required deposit. Con Edison lost millions of dollars in the process. She told me the story many years ago, but I never forgot it. Some may call it a coincidence, but I believe, with Jung, that there are no coincidences, only synchronized events.

If Jesus was plentiful in the dispensation of justice, he was equally plentiful in the dispensation of compassion. Justice and compassion are represented by the fourth and fifth Sephira of the Tree of Life, Chesed and Geburah. He was moved by the suffering and the pain he constantly encountered. His work as a healer was based on this deep compassion. But behind the compassion was always his will: Chesed in harmony with Geburah. Matthew tells us that after Jesus came down from the mount, after the sermon, great crowds followed him. Among them was a leper, who came to Jesus and, kneeling before him, said, "Lord, if you choose, you can make me clean." Jesus stretched out his hand and touched the leper, saying, "I do choose. Be made clean!" Immediately, the man's leprosy was cleansed (Matt. 8:1). By saying, "I do choose," Jesus was establishing his will to heal the leper. He exhibited the same compassion tempered by will in his healings of the centurion's servant, Peter's mother-in-law, and many others.

Jesus's many miracles, related in the four gospels, were based on the perfect balance of the appropriate spheres of the Tree of Life. According to John, Jesus's first public miracle was turning the water into wine at the wedding in Cana. Jesus, his mother, and his disciples had been invited to the wedding. When the wine was finished, Mary pointed out to Jesus that the hosts had run out of wine. He told her that his time had not yet come, but Mary knew her son well and was sure he would help with the problem. She therefore instructed the servants to do whatever Jesus said. Nearby were six stone jars for the Jewish rites of purification, each holding twenty or thirty gallons. Jesus asked the servants to fill the jars with water. After they had done so, he told them to draw some of the liquid out and take it to the chief steward. When the steward tasted the water that had become wine, he told the bridegroom that while others served the best wine first, he had kept the best wine for last.

The transformation of water into wine falls within the realm of Yesod, the ninth Sephira. This sphere rules the water element and all liquids. It is also the sphere of illusion, where the power of mind rules over the senses. Jesus did not change the water into wine. What he did was use the power of his mind, focused on Yesod, to give the water the illusory look and taste of wine. To anyone who tasted this mentally charged liquid it was the best of wines, but in reality it was still water.

The wine feat was repeated with the feeding of the multitudes with five loaves of bread and a few fish. Everyone saw the bread and the fish multiply. They all ate and were filled. There were even leftovers, but it was all the work of a kabbalistic combination between Sephiroth. This was not a trick. It was the magnificent accomplishment of a supreme kabbalist.

Jesus often used spiritually significant stories called parables to illustrate his teachings. Some biblical scholars believe that Jesus's parables, usually stories about simple daily events, represent a distinct literary style. A parable is a metaphor or simile drawn from nature or common life that stimulates the imagination of the listener to examine and interpret its meaning. As a teaching method, it draws parallels with the listener's familiar surroundings, making profound truths easier to understand.

Parables do not appear in the Hebrew Bible except in the works of Solomon, who is credited with inventing them. The Hebrew word for parable is *mashal*. This word has many meanings including "proverb," "riddle," "sayings of the wise," as well as "parable." The rabbis, by employing a series of complicated wordplays, portrayed Solomon as the inventor of parables. Solomon wrote many proverbs, and since proverbs and parables are defined by the word mashal, they are deemed one and the same. The rabbis interpreted Ecclesiastes 12:9 as referring to Solomon: "Besides being wise, the Teacher also taught the people knowledge, weighing and studying and arranging many proverbs (parables)." The teacher in this quotation is Solomon, but Jesus, also a teacher, used the mashal to teach people knowledge as Solomon had done centuries earlier.

Parables are a very Jewish way of storytelling. They have no real parallel in any other literature. They are not even common in early Christian writings or in Greek literature, but they are abundant in the rabbinical tradition. In the times of Jesus they were a very common way of explaining the sacred texts and the Torah.

Jesus used parables to explain the nature of the kingdom of God and how it could be gained. There are dozens of parables in the gospels, each one filled with a wealth of similes and allegories. Among the most famous are the parables of the Ten Virgins and of the Ten Talents. The number ten is, again, a veiled allusion to the ten Sephiroth.

In the parable of the Ten Virgins, Jesus alludes to the importance of remaining alert to his call. Here he is represented as the Bridegroom. In this story, told in Matthew 25:1–13, Jesus likened the kingdom of heaven unto ten virgins, who took their lamps and went forth to meet the Bridegroom. Five of them were wise and five were foolish. The wise ones brought oil inside their lamps, but the foolish ones did not. When the Bridegroom came, the wise virgins went in with him to be married and the door to the wedding chamber was shut. The foolish ones had to go and buy oil for their lamps. When they returned and knocked on the Bridegroom's door he would not open it and said he did not know them. Jesus adds at the end of the parable: "Watch therefore, for you know neither the day nor the hour wherein the Son of Man (Jesus) comes."

In the Tree of Life, the Bridegroom is identified with the six Sephiroth below the upper triad. These Sephiroth are Chesed, Geburah, Tiphareth, Netzach, Hod, and Yesod, but the Bridegroom pertains especially to Tiphareth, Jesus' sphere. The collective name of the six Sephiroth is Zauir Anpin, Microprosopus, the Lesser Countenance, the Bridegroom. Kether, the first Sephira, is known as Arik Anpin, Macroprosopus, the Vast Countenance. Kether, the Vast Countenance, emanates Chokmah, the Supernal Father, also known as Abba, which means "father" in Hebrew. Binah, the third Sephira, is then emanated. She is the Supernal Mother, Aima. When these two Sephiroth unite they form the Elohim and produce an offspring, the Son, Zauir Anpin, Microprosopus, the Lesser Countenance, whose solar energies are concentrated in Tiphareth. Jesus identifies himself as the Son, the Bridegroom mentioned in the parable of the Ten Virgins.

The five wise virgins are the five partzufim of the Tree of Life and are further identified as the Bride, Malkuth, the tenth sphere, and the spouse of Zauir Anpin.

We can see in this parable a distinct reference to the Sephiroth of the Tree of Life, revealing Jesus's profound knowledge of the Kabbalah and its great importance in his teachings.

Jesus always spoke to the crowds in parables, but not to his disciples. When his disciples asked him why he used parables to instruct the common people, Jesus said, "To you it has been given to know the secrets of the kingdom, but to them it has not been given. The reason I speak to them in parables is that 'seeing they do not perceive, and hearing they do not listen nor understand.'" Here Jesus was quoting the prophet Isaiah, who had said the same thing (Matt. 13:10). Later on, Matthew himself explains that Jesus spoke in parables to fulfill David's prophecy in Psalm 78:2: "I will open my mouth to speak in parables; I will proclaim what has been hidden from the foundation of the world"

(Matt. 13:35). Therefore to speak in parables was another way Jesus identified himself with David, the Messiah.

Jesus often sought to teach his disciples through miracles. He continuously stressed the importance of faith (willpower) with each portent. In one instance, the disciples were on a boat that was being battered by the waves and tossed around by the wind. Jesus came to them walking on the water. The disciples were terrified, as they thought Jesus was a ghost. Jesus identified himself saying, "It is I, do not be afraid." Peter said to him, "Lord, if it is you, command me to come to you on the water." Jesus answered, "Come." Peter got out of the boat and started walking on the water, but then, seeing that the winds were strong, he became frightened and began to sink. He called out to Jesus to save him, and Jesus said, "You of little faith, why did you doubt?"

On another occasion, he was walking with his disciples along a road. As he was hungry, he approached a fig tree and looked for fruit among the leaves but found none. He immediately cursed the tree for its barrenness and the tree withered at once. When his disciples asked him how this was done, Jesus said, "Truly I tell you, if you have faith and do not doubt, not only will you do what has been done to the fig tree, but even if you say to this mountain, 'Be lifted up and thrown into the sea,' it will be done. Whatever you ask in prayer with faith you will receive" (Matt. 21:21).

Jesus was not speaking metaphorically in this teaching. He truly meant that the mountain could be thrown into the sea if the command was given with "faith." He was referring to the immense power of the human mind when it is directly connected with the universal force that is God. This is a very essential and intrinsic part of the kabbalistic teachings. Everything is possible if the faith (the will) of the individual is so unshakable as to brook no denial. The willpower, linked to the immense cosmic energy, can channel this awesome force and direct it to whatever the person wishes to accomplish. That is how "miracles" can happen.

I had the opportunity to test this teaching of Jesus when I applied to work as an English editor for the United Nations in Vienna. When I was called for a personal interview at the United Nations Headquarters in New York, there were twenty-one applicants waiting, all vying for the same post, and most of them much better qualified than myself. Remembering Jesus's words on the power of faith, I took a deep breath, concentrated fully on why I was there, and said to myself, "This job is mine. I do not know why these people are here. They are wasting their time. This job is mine." There was absolutely no doubt in my mind that I was going to get the appointment I wanted. I was so sure I would get the job, I picked up a magazine and forgot all about the interview. I was totally relaxed and completely confident. I just knew the post was mine. Several hours later, I went in for my interview. The two persons who were present looked at my resume, asked a few questions, and then one of them asked suddenly, "How soon can you leave for Vienna?" A few weeks later, I was on my way to Austria.

There seems to be a formula in this teaching of Jesus. It is composed of two major ingredients: one is faith and the other is lack of doubt. That is why Jesus said to Peter, "You of little faith. Why did you doubt?" Again, when he cursed the fig tree, he said to his disciples, "If you have faith and do not doubt, you can do this and much more." During my United Nations interview, I had total faith I would get the appointment. I had no doubt I would. Therefore I got the job.

Throughout the four gospels, we are constantly faced with Jesus's great self-assurance. He is totally convinced he can heal people, he can turn water into wine, he can walk on water, he can feed thousands with a few fish and a few loaves of bread. He has no doubts as to his powers, his divine mission, his identity as the Messiah. He projects such an immensity of faith that he transcends the physical world and merges with the divine. Because he believes he can accomplish these miracles and has no doubt, he succeeds. And the most astonishing aspect of this teaching is that he does not claim these powers as strictly his own; rather, he tells his disciples, and us, through the disciples, that we can all accomplish the same miracles. At no time in the gospels does he say that he is the only one who can do miracles. Neither does he claim that he is the only Son of God, for he continuously tells his disciples, "Ask your Father for these things and He will give them to you." In saying this, he is telling us that the "Father," Kether, Macroprosopus, is the father of all, and that we can all aspire to the powers embodied in the Tree of Life.

Jesus, as the Teacher, is God's greatest gift to the world. It is a cosmic illumination. Jesus opens the Tree of Life for us and makes it available to everyone. Nowhere is this more clear than in Jesus's teaching of the Paternoster.

II

THE PATERNOSTER

Whenever you stand praying, forgive,
if you have anything against anyone;
so that your Father in heaven may
also forgive your trespasses.

—JESUS, MARK 11:25

The Paternoster (the Our Father or Lord's Prayer) has been described as the perfect prayer by Christian theologians. After the rite of baptism, it is the best-known bond of unity among Christians of every tradition and is recited in all ecumenical gatherings. It is an all-encompassing petition where every human need is placed in perfect trust on the hands of a divine progenitor whose love and compassion will ensure that those needs will be met. It is significant that this petition is not a plea. The Paternoster does not "beg" for help or for mercy. It tells God exactly what is needed of him. This is very characteristic of Jesus's teachings, where faith is absolute and there is no doubt about the outcome of a prayer or an act of will. Jesus's faith in God's infinite mercy is such that he has no doubt that the prayer will be answered. That is why he tells God what is wanted of him in the Paternoster. This echoes his triple teachings: "Ask and it shall be given you, seek and you shall find, knock and it shall be opened unto you" (Matt. 6:9).

Following is a contemporary version of the Paternoster used in Catholic and Protestant youth services. It was approved by an international and ecumenical body known as the International Consultation on English Texts.

Our Father in heaven, holy be your name.
Your kingdom come. Your will be done on earth as in heaven.
Give us today our daily bread.
Forgive us our sins, as we forgive those who sin against us.
Do not bring us to the test, but deliver us from evil.
For the kingdom, the power and the glory
Are yours now and forever. Amen.

The Paternoster appears only in the gospels of Matthew (6:9–13) and Luke (11:1–4). The two gospels differ in the internal structure of the prayer. The segment that says "Your kingdom come, your will be done" is found in Matthew but not in Luke. Some modern biblical translations use "And do not bring us to the time of trial (or test)" instead of "Do not lead us into temptation." The "time of trial" is preferred because it implies conflict with spiritual powers and human adversaries. It is also a truer version of the original Aramaic.

"Our daily bread" refers to both material and spiritual needs. Thus "material bread" may include not only food but other necessities, such as shelter and financial help. "Spiritual bread" refers to love, peace, and other spiritual essentials.

The closing doxology of the Paternoster is only a footnote in most standard versions of the Bible, although the St. James version cites it fully in the Gospel of Matthew. This famous end of the Paternoster is recited by the officiating priest and the congregation during Catholic mass, but it is not mentioned by most Catholics during their private recital of the prayer. Most Protestants include the doxology when they pray the Paternoster. The doxology says, "For yours is the kingdom and the power and the glory forever. Amen."

A doxology is a hymn or formula of praise to God. The closing doxology of the Paternoster was incorporated into the Lord's Prayer as early as the first century CE, when it appeared in the Didache, a brief manual of instruction for converts to Christianity.

Following is the Aramaic version of the Paternoster (see Charlesworth, *Lord's Prayer*) as it must have been originally given by Jesus to his disciples. The Aramaic has been transliterated to aid in the actual pronunciation of the prayer:

PATER NOSTER IN ARAMAIC

Avvon d-bish-maiya, nith-quaddash shimmukh.
Tih-teh mal-kutukh. Nih-weh shiw-yanukh:
Ei-chana d'bish-maiya: ap b'ar-ah.
Haw lan lakh-ma d'soonqa-nan yoo-mana.
O'shwooq lan kho-bein:
Ei-chana d'ap kh'nan shwiq-qan l'khaya-ween.
Oo'la te-ellan l'niss-yoona:
Il-la pash-shan min beesha.
Mid-til de-di-lukh hai mal-kutha
Oo kai-la oo tush-bookh-ta
L'alam al-mein. Aa-meen.

ENGLISH TRANSLATION
FROM THE ARAMAIC

Our heavenly Father, hallowed is your name.
Your Kingdom is come. Your will is done,
As in heaven so also on earth.
Give us the bread of our daily need.
And leave us serene,
Just as we allow others serenity.
And do not pass us through trial,
Except separate us from the evil one.
For yours is the Kingdom,
The Power and the Glory
To the end of the universe, of all the universes. Amen.

The Paternoster has seven petitions, modeled on the psalms. The first three are concerned with the glory of God:

Our heavenly father,
1. Hallowed is your name.
2. Your Kingdom is come.
3. Your will is done, as in heaven so also on earth.

You will notice that in the translation of the Aramaic version these three petitions are in the present. God's name *is* hallowed, his Kingdom *is* come and his will *is* done. In the standard biblical versions, this segment is in the future—God's name be hallowed, his kingdom come, his will be done.

The emphasis on the present in the Aramaic version is of vital importance because it underlines Jesus's teaching of the paramount relevance of the Now in all petitions to God and all acts of will. Things must happen Now for Jesus, because Now implies the petition has already been granted. God's name is always hallowed, his kingdom always comes, and his will is always done. Not in the future, but Now and always. This emphasis on the present is missing in the traditional versions of the Bible, diminishing significantly the power of the prayer.

The remaining four petitions are requests for divine assistance to humanity:

4. Give us the bread for our daily need.
5. And leave us serene, just as we allow others serenity.
6. And do not pass us through trial,
7. Except separate us from the evil one.

The fifth petition is careful in reminding God that we have allowed serenity to others. This means we have forgiven others for their offenses, granting them peace thereby. Therefore we are worthy to receive God's forgiveness for our own sins. That is why Jesus advises his disciples to forgive their debtors before they pray.

The prayer then closes with the doxology, glorifying God:

For yours is the Kingdom, the Power and the Glory to the end
of the universe, of all universes. Amen.

This remarkable hymn, in the original Aramaic, goes beyond "forever and ever." The person who wrote it reveals a profound knowledge of cosmology, for he knows that there are other universes, something astrophysicists have only recently discovered. It is the closing doxology of the Paternoster that confirms Jesus's position as a consummate kabbalist. The Kingdom, the Power, and the Glory refer to the tenth, seventh, and eighth Sephiroth of the Tree of Life: Malkuth, the Kingdom (10), Netzach, the Power (7); and Hod, the Glory (8). The universes Jesus speaks about in the doxology are the four worlds emanated from God during creation: Atziluth, Briah, Yetzirah, and Assiah. Clearly, the author of the Paternoster was very familiar with the Tree of Life.

It is significant that the doxology does not appear in the gospels. The reason for this obvious omission is that the closing hymn is a kabbalistic teaching, and as such it is part of Jesus' secret oral teachings to his disciples. The people who wrote the Didache may have been unfamiliar with the secrecy of these teachings and simply reinstated the doxology to the prayer.

If the closing doxology is a kabbalistic revelation, the rest of the Paternoster is an equally potent kabbalistic formula. Let us find the Tree of Life in the Prayer.

Kether (1)—*Our heavenly father*—Kether represents the creative force, as it emanates downward to create the world. As such it is the Supernal Father.

Chokmah (2)—*Hallowed is*—Chokmah represents the Creator's light, his power to bestow his cosmic energy; therefore, it refers to God's holiness.

Binah (3)—*Your name*—In Binah we find for the first time the power of God's creative essence in the name of Elohim, a male and a female principle united for the purpose of manifestation.

Malkuth (10)—*Your Kingdom is come*—Malkuth is the Kingdom, the consolidation of the Godhead's light on the material world. Creation is accomplished.

Daath (0)—*Your will is done*—Daath is the invisible Sephira. It symbolizes knowledge, the result of the union between wisdom (Chokmah) and understanding (Binah). It is in this knowledge that God's will is founded.

Kether (1)—*As in heaven*—Kether represents the unmanifested light of the Creator. As such it is equated with heaven, the infinite.

Malkuth (10)—*So also on earth*—Malkuth also symbolizes earth, the physical world.

Chesed (4)—*Give us the bread for our daily need*—Chesed is the sphere of mercy and compassion and love. Therefore it is only through Chesed that we can receive God's bounties.

Geburah (5)—*And leave us serene*—Geburah is justice. We ask God to forgive us as a judge releases and therefore forgives a prisoner who is found innocent.

Tiphareth (6)—*Just as we allow others serenity*—Tiphareth is beauty. It is in the beauty of our souls that we can find the mercy to forgive those who have offended us, and our forgiveness of those offenses makes us worthy of Geburah's justice.

Yesod (9)—*And do not pass through trial, except separate us from the evil one*—Yesod is foundation. It may be likened to the root of all evil and of all good. It is also ascribed to the sexual organs, often a source of trial and temptation to humanity.

Malkuth (10)—*For yours is the Kingdom*—Here Malkuth, the kingdom of earth, is returned to God, to whom it rightfully belongs as the Creator.

Netzach (7)—*And the Power*—Netzach represents victory, the power of achievement, of triumph on every level.

Hod (8)—*And the Glory*—Hod is the sphere where all things coalesce and are accomplished. It is the glory of Netzach's victory over all trials and tribulations.

Kether (1)—*To the end of the universe, of all the universes*—Here we recognize that eventually all must return to the Creator, who emanated this and all other universes.

In the Paternoster the Tree of Life is traversed starting with the first three Sephiroth to assert God's divinity and the power of his will. We immediately connect with the tenth and last Sephira, to "earth" the divine power and bring creation into fruition. The next three spheres (4, 5, and 6) are contacted next to ensure material and spiritual comforts as well as peace of mind. Then we turn our attention to physical and spiritual protection from all harm through the ninth sphere. Now that our needs have been fulfilled, we reiterate God's power and glory and return the Kingdom, including ourselves and all that we have received, unto the Creator. We end the prayer by accepting that all of creation will return to God at the completion of his plan.

As we can see in Table 1, the Tree of Life is identified with the human body. The first Sephira is ascribed the crown of the head; the second pertains to the right side of the face; the third to the left side of the face; the fourth to the right arm and shoulder; the fifth to the left arm and shoulder; the sixth to the heart; the seventh to the right thigh and hip; the eighth to the left thigh and hip; the ninth to the genital organs; and the tenth to the feet. Those body parts pertain to the tree when we look at it as a diagram, that is, from outside the tree. But when we try to locate the various Sephiroth in our bodies, the order is reversed. As we become the tree, the right spheres (Chokmah, Chesed, and Netzach) are found on the left side of the body, and the left spheres (Binah, Geburah, and Hod) are found on the right. The middle spheres retain their positions.

The Paternoster should be said while standing. The most dynamic way to recite the prayer and acquire its true powers is to connect it to the various Sephiroth as we say the prayer. To do this, we touch each part of the body pertaining to the sphere ascribed to each segment or petition of the Paternoster. We then recite that petition as follows:

Touch the top of the head (Kether) and say, *Our heavenly Father.*

Touch the left cheek (Chokmah) and say, *Hallowed is.*

Touch the right cheek (Binah) and say, *Your name.*

Point to the feet (Malkuth) and say, *Your Kingdom is come.*

Touch the throat (Daath) and say, *Your will is done.*

Touch the top of the head (Kether) and say, *As in heaven.*

Point to the feet (Malkuth) and say, *So also on earth.*

Touch the left shoulder (Chesed) and say, *Give us the bread for our daily need.*

Touch the right shoulder (Geburah) and say, *And leave us serene.*

Touch the center of the chest (Tiphareth) and say, *Just as we allow others serenity.*

Point to the genital area (Yesod) and say, *And do not pass us through trial, except separate us from the evil one.*

Point to the feet (Malkuth) and say, *For yours is the Kingdom.*

Touch the left hip (Netzach) and say, *And the Power.*

Touch the right hip (Hod) and say, *And the Glory.*

Touch the top of the head again (Kether) and say, *To the end of the universe, of all the universes. Amen.*

This is known as the kabbalistic Paternoster. Anyone who recites this prayer daily, connecting it with the ten Sephiroth in the manner described, will experience an immediate and very positive change in his or her life. The entire body becomes vibrant and filled with strength and vitality. More important still, things seem to fall in their proper place, priorities are reassessed, and a great sense of inner peace and self-control are immediately felt. The prayer will not stop problems from arising, but it will help to solve them.

As you become more familiar with this small ritual, you may want to add the power of visualization to the prayer. To this end, you may begin visualizing the telesmatic images associated with each sphere as you say the prayer. These images are given in Table 1. This will multiply tenfold the power of the prayer as it will integrate it to your deep unconscious where these images are kept.

If you are a Christian and know the Paternoster by heart and do not want to use the Aramaic version given here, you can still get excellent results by reciting the prayer as you know it but connecting it with the ten Sephiroth.

In modern times, the Paternoster reflects the needs of a community and it is based on eschatological hope, that is, the praying for the completion of God's final plan. Eschatology is a branch of theology that deals with the end or finality of things, such as death and immortality. The petitions concerning forgiveness, temptation, and deliverance from evil are interpreted by the Christian churches in relation with the end times. The prayer is considered a synthesis of Christian faith. Its balanced structure makes it an expression of the biblical hierarchy of values, where the things of God come first, followed by human concerns.

Jesus's vision, as exemplified in the Paternoster, is that of a total union with God. This unity portends that what is being asked of the Creator has already taken place because the one reciting the prayer has complete faith, untainted by doubt, that his request has been granted before the words have been uttered. That is implied in God's omniscient wisdom and understanding, represented by Kether, Chokmah, and Binah: *Our heavenly Father, hallowed is your name.*

12

THE KEYS OF
THE KINGDOM

And I will give you the keys
of the kingdom of heaven . . .
—JESUS, MATTHEW 16:19

The word *mitzvah* means "commandment" or "precept." It is derived from the Hebrew verb *zavah*, "to establish" or "to command." According to an ancient tradition, the Torah or Law, given by God to Moses, includes 613 *mitzvoth* (plural). Of these commandments, 365 are negative and prohibit certain acts, expressed as "thou shall not." They symbolize the days of the year. The remaining 248 commandments are positive and are expressed as "thou shall." These correspond to different parts of the body. The Jewish scholar Maimonides was the first to derive the full number of mitzvoth from the Torah in the twelfth century. Before Maimonides, no one had been able to determine the actual number of commandments in the Torah because they are scattered between the books of Exodus, Leviticus, and Deuteronomy.

The best known of the 613 mitzvoth of the Torah are the Ten Commandments that God gave to Moses on Mount Sinai. They are also known as the Decalogue. According to Exodus 31:18, the Ten Commandments were inscribed on two stone tablets by God himself. They were destroyed by Moses in a fit of anger because of the Israelites' abandonment of their faith. Later he was commanded by God to prepare a new set of tablets on which the Godhead inscribed the Commandments anew. The new tablets were kept in the Ark of the

Covenant together with Aaron's rod and a pot of manna, the honeyed wafers that rained from heaven to feed the Hebrews during their forty-year sojourn in the desert.

There are two versions of the Decalogue given in the scriptures. One is given in Exodus 20:1–17 and the other in Deuteronomy 5:6–21. The substance of the commandments is the same in both accounts, but the Exodus version gives a religious rather than a humanitarian motive for observing the Sabbath. Also, in the prohibition of covetousness, it classifies a man's wife with the rest of his possessions, instead of separately, as in the Deuteronomy account.

Because the Decalogue was given before the other parts of the covenant between God and the Hebrews, it had a unique status in ancient Israel. The Ten Commandments formed the basis of all of Israel's legislation and are frequently cited in the Old Testament, notably in Leviticus 19:3–4, Psalm 15:2–5, Jeremiah 7:9, and Hosea 4:2.

The Covenant between God and Israel was ratified when Moses read the Book of the Covenant in the hearing of the people and they said, "All that the Lord has spoken we will do and be obedient." Moses then sprinkled the people with the blood of sacrificed oxen and said, "Behold, the blood of the covenant which the Lord has made with you according to all these words." This is related in Exodus 24:7–8 and underlines the importance that blood had in all covenants with the Deity.

Most modern scholars believe that the Book of the Covenant included a section from Exodus 20:23 to 23:33, but no one knows the full scope of this book.

The Ten Commandments are enumerated differently in Judaism and Christianity. In the Jewish tradition they are:

1. I am the Lord your God. (Known as the Prologue.)

2. You shall not have any other gods before me, you shall not make any graven images nor serve them.

3. You shall not take the name of the Lord your God in vain.

4. Remember the Sabbath, to keep it holy. Six days you shall labor but the seventh day is the Sabbath of the Lord your God. In it you shall not do any work: you, your family, servants or your cattle.

5. Honor your father and your mother.

6. You shall not murder.

7. You shall not steal.

8. You shall not commit adultery.

9. You shall not bear false witness against your neighbor.

10. You shall not covet your neighbor's wife or anything that is your neighbor's.

Of these commandments or mitzvoth, two are positive and seven are negative. The positive are the fourth and the fifth. The rest are negative, except the Prologue, where the Deity introduces himself as the Lord God of Israel.

Most Protestant and Orthodox Christians combine the Prologue and the prohibition of the worship of other deities as the first commandment. The prohibition of graven images and idolatry is the second. The rest of the commandments follow the traditional Jewish enumeration.

Roman Catholics and Lutherans follow the enumeration suggested by fourth century theologian Saint Augustine (see St. Augustine, *Confessions*). In this enumeration, the Prologue and the prohibitions regarding the worship of other deities are the first commandment. The last commandment is divided into two, namely, the coveting of a neighbor's wife and the coveting of his property. The commandment that prohibits the making of graven images and worshipping them is not included in the Catholic Decalogue. Therefore, unlike Protestants, who list this commandment and shun all images, Catholics have images of Jesus, Mary, angels, and various saints. These images are not worshipped but seen as a focus for Christian faith. Many Catholics defend their use of images, commenting that even the Jews, who shied away from all graven forms, placed the images of two cherubim on the sides of the Ark of the Covenant. Following are the Catholic Ten Commandments:

1. I am the Lord your God. You shall have no other gods before me.

2. You shall not take the name of the Lord your God in vain.

3. Remember to observe the Sabbath.

4. Honor your father and mother.

5. You shall not kill.

6. You shall not commit adultery.

7. You shall not steal.

8. You shall not bear false testimony against your neighbor.

9. You shall not covet your neighbor's wife.

10. You shall not covet anything that is your neighbor's.

Saint Thomas Aquinas and Saint Bonaventure believed that the commandments are part of nature's laws and as such are knowable to all thinking people. They maintained that God revealed the commandments to Moses to remind humankind of its obligations, which were forgotten because of original sin. Both Tertullian and Saint Augustine expressed a similar idea, namely, that the commandments had already been engraved in the human heart before they were hewn on tablets of stone.

Although other ancient religious systems, such as the Babylonian and the Egyptian, had codes of moral conduct, the Ten Commandments differ strongly from them in their explicit monotheism.

In the New Testament, all the commandments are mentioned, but never in a list of ten. Although Jesus said he had not come to destroy the law but to fulfill it, he nevertheless sought to reinterpret the commandments in his own special way. Thus he allowed his disciples to pluck grain from the fields to eat on the Sabbath and healed a man's withered hand on that most holy of days. Then he told the Pharisees, who were waiting to condemn him, that it was lawful to do good on the Sabbath. He expanded on the commandment that prohibits adultery, saying that whoever looks at a woman with lust has already committed adultery with her in his heart. Likewise, he added to the commandment prohibiting murder, saying that whoever is angry with another without cause is also endangering his soul. And he cautioned also on the commandment forbidding to take God's name in vain, saying that it is better not to swear at all, whether rightly or falsely. He also reinterpreted several of the 613 statutes, including the Mosaic Law that allows a man to divorce his wife. He explained that Moses had given the Jews that law because of the hardness of their hearts, but that it was wrong for a man to divorce his wife except for sexual immorality.

The teachings of Jesus parallel the Ten Commandments. Most of them are also divided into positive and negative mitzvoh but some are neither, being rather sets of instructions on moral behavior. The core of these teachings number thirty-two, and are keyed to the thirty-two paths of the Tree of Life.

The first ten of these teachings are identified with the ten Sephiroth of the Tree of Life which, as we have seen, are also the first ten Paths of the tree.

It is to be noted that nowhere in the Ten Commandments does God ask Israel to love him. Love is not a mitzvah. God, in his infinite wisdom, knows he cannot demand love from a human being. Love must be given freely or not at all. Jesus, however, places the love of God above all things and instructs his disciples on the importance of this divine love. It is the first and most essential of his commandments. Following are Jesus's Ten Commandments, identified with the ten Sephiroth of the Tree of Life:

1. Kether—Love God with all your heart, your soul and your mind.

2. Chokmah—Love your neighbor as you love yourself.

3. Binah—Love your enemies, bless those who curse you, do good to those who hate you and pray for those who persecute you.

4. Chesed—When you give alms, be sure that your left hand does not know what your right hand is doing.

5. Geburah—Do not judge so you will not be judged.

6. Tiphareth—Do not set your light under a basket but on a candle holder so that your entire house will be illuminated.

7. Netzach— Do not cast pearls before swine.

8. Hod—Ask and it shall be given unto you, seek and you shall find, knock and it shall be opened unto you.

9. Yesod—Enter through the narrow gate because wide is the gate that leads to destruction.

10. Malkuth—I will give you the keys of the kingdom of heaven and whatever you bind on earth will be bound in heaven, and whatever you loose on earth will be loosed in heaven.

    Daath—This is the hidden sphere, Knowledge. Although it is not numbered, it also has a teaching of Jesus associated with it. The teaching is: There is nothing covered that will not be uncovered nor hidden that will not be revealed.

As we saw earlier, some of Jesus's commandments are positive, some are negative, and some are instructions or revelations. You will notice that the first three commandments of Jesus are positive and are all concerned with love.

The first commandment tells us to love God with all our hearts, souls, and minds. This commandment is connected with Kether because this Sephira is where the divine energy that we know as God resides. Here Jesus is revealing to us that God is love and that in order to connect with his infinite power we have to love him in return. Nothing is possible, Jesus is telling us, without this divine connection. We must love God totally, surrender ourselves to his wisdom and compassion and accept his decisions as our own. This is the first step to empowerment. When we love God completely, we do his will gladly, which means embracing and obeying each of his commandments. When we do this we become part of his covenant and our will is one with his. There is true wisdom here because when our wills are one with God's there is nothing we cannot accomplish. We have fused our minds, hearts, and souls with the mind, the heart, and the soul of the universe.

Angels, which have been defined as God's ideas, have limited willpower but their love for their creator is so great that even that limited will is placed at his disposal. Human beings, on the other hand, have total free will. We can do what we want, both good and evil acts. It is our choice, given to us through God's unbounded mercies at the very beginning of creation. God gave us this choice of free will because he wants us to decide for ourselves which course of action we are to follow. Through the Ten Commandments and the 613 statutes in the Old Testament he gave us a guide to help us in our evolutionary path. It is up to us to follow or not to follow this guide. If we do we will find the road much easier to travel.

As we have seen, the Paternoster was modeled after the Psalms. Jesus, who believed himself to be the Messiah, identified totally with David, the reputed author of most of the Psalms. One of the most famous of these songs of praise is Psalm 91. This psalm is especially noteworthy in that it is divided into three parts. In the first part (versicles 1–2), the psalmist expresses his trust in God and his powerful protection. In the second part (versicles 2–13), he describes the various ways in which God's protection works. In the third part (versicles 14–16), it is God himself who speaks through the psalmist, saying:

> Those who love me I will deliver;
> I will protect those who know my name.

When they call to me, I will answer them.
I will be with them in trouble,
I will rescue them and honor them.
With long life I will satisfy them,
And show them my salvation.

It is clear through this passage that loving God and knowing his name has definite advantages. According to Psalm 91, a person who loves God will enjoy God's protection and will live a long life full of honors. Furthermore, when they call on God for help, he will answer them, which is the same thing as saying God will grant their wishes. All that is necessary is to love God and to know his name. That is the reason why Jesus asks his disciples to love God with all their hearts, their souls, and their minds.

As we have seen, God has many names, but the name that must be known in Psalm 91 is the name connected with Kether, the first sphere of the Tree of Life, the sphere where God's light first becomes manifested as the created universe. This name is Eheieh, the Father, the Creator.

Once the name is known, the person must seek to fill his heart, soul, and mind with love for his creator. Gratitude for the gift of life and consciousness, appreciation for the wonders of the earth and of the universe, recognition that the ills plaguing the world are not God's creation but our own, and awareness of the infinite possibilities that are at our disposal for transforming and bettering our lives through the power of will—all of these things can go a long way in planting the seed of love in our beings for the Creative Force that made them all possible. This is the seed of *devvekut*, total devotion to God. The next step is to return the gift of willpower to God.

There is a simple ritual that can be used to follow this first commandment of Jesus. On the day of the New Moon, the person wishing to do this ritual of devvekut, that is, embracing God and his will, dresses in white and faces the east, where the sun rises every morning. He or she must be barefoot and perfectly clean. The person opens his arms widely and says,

THE KEYS OF THE KINGDOM

My Creator and Father, AHIH (Eheieh), infinite light of the cosmos, from this day onward I pledge my love and surrender my will to you. I return it to you as you gave it to me on my creation. I wish to be one with you. Whatever you will is my will, whether or not it benefits me. I give you my love as my last act of free will. Into your divine hands I entrust my life, my body, my mind, and my soul. Your will, which is my will, be done now and forever to the end of this universe and all the universes. Amen.

After this short ritual the person resumes his normal life but with an important difference. Being empowered by God's will, whatever this person desires will come to pass, provided he obeys God's laws and has total faith (no doubts) in the outcome of his desire. However, as the person has embraced God's will, whenever something that is desired does not take place or when negative things happen, these events must also be accepted without question as God's will. It will be found, however, that more positive than negative things will happen, and as time passes and the person's link with the divine becomes stronger, truly miraculous events will take place in his life.

The second of Jesus's commandments says, "Love your neighbor as you love yourself." It is identified with the second Sephira of the Tree of Life because in the same way Chokmah flows from Kether, so does love flow from God unto those around us. The "neighbor" symbolizes all of humanity and all of the created universe. Therefore we must love everything that exists in the same measure as we love ourselves.

The third commandment is an extension of the second. We must love all that exists including those who hate us and do evil unto us. This love implies understanding of their motives. That is why this commandment is associated with the third Sephira, Binah, which means understanding. It is "understandably" difficult to love those who are our enemies, though this love need not be devotion but acceptance of the right of these people to survive for they are also part of the creation which must be sacred to us. In the light of the Law of Three, which we already discussed, we leave the punishment of those who ill treat us in the hands of the Creative Force of the universe, and justice will be done on our behalf multiplied by three. Moreover, if we bless those who curse us, do good unto those who hate us, and pray for those who persecute us, we receive the Creator's blessings, also multiplied by three. It is no coincidence that the Sephira connected with this commandment of Jesus is the third sphere.

Daath, the hidden sphere that connects Chokmah and Binah, means knowledge. The teaching identified with Daath is, "There is nothing covered that will not be uncovered nor hidden that will not be revealed." It is not a commandment but an instruction. It refers to the hidden knowledge in Daath that will be revealed through the various keys.

Commandments four to nine are mitzvoth. Of these, four to seven are negative and eight and nine are positive. All these commandments are secret keys, like the first three. If followed, they will help the individual in his personal quests.

The last seven Sephiroth of the Tree of Life are used to acquire things in the material world. In other words, they are used for petitions. The first three, known as the Supernals, are never used for material purposes. The Sephiroth on the left and right-hand columns must be used in conjunction with their opposites during rituals and meditations for the purpose of accomplishing something. This is necessary to ensure that the tree is always in balance. The Sephiroth on the Middle Pillar are used alone.

For example, any work that is done on Chesed, the fourth Sephira, must be done in conjunction with work with the fifth, Geburah, which lies opposite to it. Likewise, any work done on the seventh Sephira, Netzach, must be done in conjunction with the eighth, Hod.

In the Paternoster, we find the same division of power as in the Tree of Life.

The fourth commandment of Jesus says, "When you give alms, be sure that your left hand does not know what your right hand is doing." As Chesed, the fourth sphere, means compassion, any alms-giving will be connected with it. Therefore this commandment is identified with Chesed.

As we saw earlier, in the Paternoster, the first three petitions are devoted to the glory of God. Nothing is asked of a personal nature. These three petitions are identified with the first three spheres of the Tree and the first three commandments of Jesus. The petitions for personal need start with the seven lower Sephiroth, identified with Jesus's commandments.

Jesus's fourth commandment is identified with Chesed, to which also belongs the petition of the Paternoster: "Give us this day our daily bread."

Chesed represents mercy, compassion, and generosity. Therefore in this sphere we ask God for "our daily bread," which includes all our material needs. Chesed is the sphere of prosperity, abundance, and long journeys. Banks, employers, and people in positions of power who may be of help to us all fall under the aegis of the fourth Sephiroth. It is here that we must work if we need a bank loan, if we want to buy a house, if we want to get a job, if we want a raise, if we want to succeed in life. But Jesus speaks of alms-giving in the commandment identified with this sphere. He tells us that when we give alms, no one must know of our good actions. This is the key to the working of this sphere. What Jesus is truly saying is that if we want the abundance and prosperity promised by this sphere, we must first give alms; we must give in order to receive. And we must do it in secret. No one must know, not even the recipient of our charity, that we have given them alms. This means that as part of the work on this sphere we must choose a person or a charity organization and send them an anonymous contribution. This contribution must be a tithe or ten percent of our earnings for a week's work. As a week has seven days, it refers to the seven Sephiroth where work is done on the tree for material gain. The tithe or ten percent is the amount mentioned in the scriptures as the perfect amount for alms. It will amount to a generous contribution, a true sacrifice on the part of the giver. It will also ensure that whatever is asked of God will be granted.

The fifth commandment of Jesus says, "Do not judge so you will not be judged." It is identified with the fifth Sephira, Geburah, which represents justice, judgment, and severity. When work for the acquisition of money or prosperity is done in Chesed, the fifth sphere must be balanced. What the fifth commandment means is that we must not be concerned with what happens to the money we have given as alms. We must not wonder if the person or institution to whom we contributed that money is worthy of our sacrifice. Once the money is sent, the matter is out of our hands.

The names of God pertaining to both Chesed and Geburah must be mentioned when the alms are given. Psalm 91 tells us that God will protect those who know his name. And his name is different in every sphere of the Tree of Life. In Chesed, his name is El. In Geburah, his name is Elohim Gebor. Therefore, when asking abundance and prosperity through Chesed, one says: "In the name of El and Elohim Gebor, I give these alms so that my petition will be fulfilled through God's will." Light a blue candle as the name of El is pronounced and a red candle with the name Elohim Gebor.

This work is best done on the New Moon or while the Moon is waxing.

The person should be clean, dressed in white, and barefoot. The reason why shoes are not worn during these rituals goes back to Moses and the Burning Bush, when he was instructed to remove his sandals as he was on holy ground. Any place where God is invoked ritualistically is holy ground, including one's home.

The Chesed ritual as described here is very simple, but extremely powerful, and is always effective.

The sphere of Geburah represents legal matters, judges, the military, war, enemies, surgeries and surgeons, firemen, policemen, and severity.

When work is necessary on this Sephira to overcome any of the problems associated with the sphere, the same ritual is used as with Chesed but the name of God in Geburah is mentioned first. Also, the red candle is lit before the blue. Alms must also be given to balance the two Sephiroth. The purpose of the ritual, that is, what is desired, must be mentioned in both rituals. For example, if the person conducting the ritual is facing a dangerous surgery, he would say: "In the name of Elohim Gebor and El, I ask that my surgery will be successful and safe. I give alms so that my petition be fulfilled through God's will." Then he lights the red candle followed by the blue. The alms must be sent immediately after the ritual.

The sixth commandment says, "Do not set your light under a basket but on a candle holder so that your entire house will be illuminated." This commandment is identified with Tiphareth, the sphere of the Sun, and represents the central light of the Tree of Life, which descends directly from Kether, God's infinite light. This cosmic light is filtered through Daath, the hidden sphere. That is why the name of God in Tiphareth is Jehovah Elo Ve Daath. Jehovah is the most sacred name of God, the Tetragrammaton. Jehovah Elo Ve Daath means that AHIH (Eheieh), God's name in Kether, the first sphere, is transmuted into IHVH through the knowledge hidden in Daath as it reaches the sixth Sephira, Tiphareth. As Kether is cosmic light undefined, Tiphareth is physical light manifested in the rays of the Sun. This light illuminates the entire solar system, nourishing each of its planets.

When Jesus tells us not to hide our light but to place it where it will illuminate our entire house, he is referring to the light of the Sun that is shared generously with all the planets of the solar system. The planets are the "entire house" Jesus mentions in this commandment.

Like the Sun, we must let our light, that is, our love, and all the shining qualities we receive from the upper spheres, shine upon all those who surround us. Tiphareth's title is Beauty. The "beauty" to which it refers is the beauty of the soul. It is the light of the human spirit and of the human mind.

From its position on the center of the tree, Tiphareth connects with eight of the other Sephiroth. The only Sephira that is not connected with Tiphareth is Malkuth, identified as the planet Earth. This happens because Malkuth is a fallen sphere where the dark shadows of the Qlippoth dwell.

Tiphareth represents wealth, good health, success, mental power, and power in general. When we need to work with this Sephira for the purpose of acquiring any of its gifts, we must share our light, our love, and our bounties in some measure, with eight different people, represented by the eight spheres to which Tiphareth is connected. These eight persons must be carefully chosen and we must then share something of ours with each of them, in accordance with their needs. These gifts may include advice, forgiveness of an offense or a debt, love, compassion, money, or anything they may need and we are in position to give.

The portion of the Paternoster assigned to Tiphareth is "as we also allow others serenity." Serenity is peace, and peace is what we will be giving these eight people with the sharing of our light.

After our gift of light and serenity, we can ask God what we want from the sphere of Tiphareth and it will be granted. The person conducting the Tiphareth ritual says, "In the name of Jehovah Elo Ve Daath, as I have given light and serenity unto others, I ask that my wishes be fulfilled through the power of God's will." Whatever is desired from the sphere must be mentioned. For example, if what is needed is good health, the person should say, "I ask that my wishes be fulfilled and good health return to my body, mind, and soul, through the power of God's will." A yellow or gold candle should then be lit.

The seventh commandment of Jesus says, "Do not cast pearls before swine." It is identified with Netzach, the seventh sphere. Netzach's title is Power, Victory. It represents love, the arts, music, enjoyment, and pleasures—everything, in fact, that makes life worth living. These are "pearls" of great price and they should not be wasted on those who would not appreciate them. The seventh commandment calls for careful scrutiny of what is asked for through this sphere. For example, if what is desired is the love of someone, the person who is doing the ritual should make sure that the object of his affections truly deserves them. This is important because Netzach is Victory and Power and whatever is asked through this sphere is instantly granted. This is one of the easiest spheres to work with because it works in conjunction with Hod, the eighth Sephira, where all thoughts coalesce and are manifested as reality. To ask for the love of someone who is unworthy through the power of Netzach is very unwise because once this love is secured, it will be forever. Should you repent later on, you will find it extremely difficult to cut these cosmic ties and you will be bound to an unwanted partner for the rest of your life. That is the reason why Jesus warns us not to cast pearls before swine. If, after careful consideration,, you still desire this person's love, all you have to do is say, "In the name of Jehovah Tzabaoth and Elohim Tzabaoth, I ask that my petition be fulfilled and this person's love is given to me through God's will." Jehovah Tzabaoth is God's name in Netzach and Elohim Tzabaoth is God's name in the opposite sphere, Hod. You then must light a green candle, which is Netzach's color, and an orange candle, which is Hod's. At this point, you must establish a link with Hod to balance the tree and get what you asked for.

The eighth commandment, identified with Hod, the eighth Sephira, is: "Ask and it shall be given unto you, seek and you shall find, knock and it shall be opened unto you." This means that you must seek the person you desire and ask for his or her love. This is a vital part of the ritual and must be done for it to be effective.

Hod's title is Glory, Splendor, and it represents papers, business matters, and contracts. To acquire anything that falls under Hod's influence, you must also connect with Netzach, its opposite, and use a strong sense of discrimination to ensure that what you desire is worthwhile. If what you wish is to enter into a business partnership with a person or an organization, you must be sure that they are trustworthy and that the business arrangement is fair to both parties. You then say, "In the name of Elohim Tzabaoth and Jehovah Tzabaoth, I ask that my wish be fulfilled and that I will consolidate this business with this person (or institution) through the power of God's will." You light an orange and a green candle and proceed to ask the person or persons involved what you wish of them.

The ninth commandment says, "Enter through the narrow gate because wide is the gate that leads to destruction." This commandment is linked with the ninth Sephira, Yesod. This is the sphere of dreams, short trips, moves, and changes. It also deals with illusions and temptations. In the Paternoster, it is associated with the segment that says, "And do not pass us through trials except separate us from the evil one." The "evil one" refers to all of our destructive tendencies, the negative side of our nature. Yesod is identified with the Moon, which, in spite of its great creative energies, is never a stable influence because of its rapid motion. The Moon stays approximately two and a half days in each sign of the zodiac. In contrast, the Sun stays thirty days in a sign and Saturn, thirty years. That is why one of Yesod's influences is change because the Moon is constantly changing. The temptations of Yesod are sore trials for human beings because here we are dealing with the sphere of illusions, where things are not what they seem to be. This is the most important Sephira for ritual work and the most dangerous. The Moon (Yesod) stands between the Earth (Malkuth) and the Sun (Tiphareth) in the Tree of Life. For that reason, the Sun of Tiphareth is in constant eclipse for the Earth. It is only through the Moon of Yesod that we receive some of the divine light. In order to receive this cosmic light fully we must travel through Yesod to Tiphareth and from Tiphareth to Kether.

But the path is fraught with obstacles and dangers, the many temptations and illusions of Yesod. That is why Jesus says, "Go through the narrow gate for wide is the gate that leads to destruction." This means we must never take the easy way out in any given situation. We must never jump to conclusions, give way to fanciful illusions, nor surrender to our destructive urges. It is better to control our fancies, make every decision with care, and reject those ideas that may lead us astray, no matter how attractive they might seem. Caution and care are the tools that will ensure our safety in the snares of Yesod. They are the "narrow gate" that Jesus refers to. Yesod's title is Foundation. This foundation must be based on clarity of mind and strength of purpose.

If you are considering an important move or change in your life, and want to accomplish it through Yesod, you must take all these things into consideration before you conduct the ritual. Ask yourself if the move or the change are the best for you, or if it would be advisable to wait for something better. If you are sure that change or move is what you want, proceed with the ritual. All you have to do is say, " In the name of Shaddai el Chai (God's name in Yesod), I ask that my wish be fulfilled and that this change (move or trip) be successful through the power of God's will." You then light a violet candle, the color of Yesod.

The tenth commandment is not a mitzvah. It is a promise that Jesus made to Peter and through him, to us. It says: "I will give you the keys of the kingdom of heaven and whatever you bind on earth will be bound on heaven, and whatever you loose on earth, will be loosed in heaven."

This commandment is identified with Malkuth, the tenth sphere, which is also the Earth. The tenth commandment is the major key to the mysteries of the Tree of Life. What Jesus is saying is that whatever is willed to happen on Earth (the material world) will find an echo in heaven (the world of mind and spirit), making what is willed manifest on the physical plane. Likewise, it is possible to "loose," to undo or change things in the material world, in the same manner. This is possible once the human will has been returned to God, making it one with that of the Creator. In order to achieve these things, we must have the keys, and these keys are Jesus's teachings embodied in his commandments. Each of these teachings have secret meanings, as we have already seen.

Malkuth's title is the Kingdom. It refers not to a material kingdom but to the kingdom of heaven. Jesus saves his most important commandment for this sphere, where all the cosmic energies are gathered and the divine and human wills are manifested. Moreover, he promises the keys of the kingdom of heaven through his teachings. Often during his preaching he said, "He who has ears, let him hear." He was referring to the secret meaning of his teachings. Whoever had "ears," that is, had the keys, would understand what he really was saying.

Malkuth is the Sephira where all physical acts take place. Thinking, visualization, meditation, and willful determinations are conducted in Yesod. That is why it is important to "enter through the narrow gate," that is, use caution in the use of the imagination. Whatever is "imagined" in Yesod with enough mental power will manifest physically in Malkuth or the physical world. We saw earlier that God first "thought" of creation before it was actually manifested. In the same manner, we can "think" ourselves into any number of situations, both positive and negative. If you constantly dwell on thoughts of poverty and misfortune, you are in fact "creating" those undesirable conditions as part of your sphere of being. If, on the other hand, you imagine yourself constantly healthy, wealthy, and happy, you will eventually see these positive changes come into your life. We mold our lives through our thoughts. Thoughts (Yesod) are continuously manifested in Malkuth (reality).

Paths 11–33 of the Tree of Life are identified with the corresponding teachings or commandments of Jesus. These Paths are not intended for actual "work" on the tree. Rather, they serve to connect the ten Sephiroth and to illuminate them. One travels the Paths between spheres but does not stop along the way. They are roads of various degrees of enlightenment. Traveling along the Paths is known as "Path Working."

Following are the twenty-two Paths that connect the ten Sephiroth and the commandments of Jesus that are identified with them.

PATH 11

This Path connects Kether (1) and Chokmah (2). The teaching of Jesus that is identified with this Path is: "With God all things are possible."

Through this teaching Jesus reiterates the importance of loving God and blending one's will with his. This teaching illuminates the first two commandments: Love God with all your heart, your mind and soul, and love your neighbor as you love yourself. If you do these two things, everything is possible for you.

PATH 12

This Path connects Kether (1) and Binah (3). The teaching associated with this Path is: "Your Father knows what you need before you ask him."

This teaching illuminates the first and the third commandments: Love God and love your enemies. God knows how difficult it is to love someone who hates you and does you harm. If you do this very difficult thing it is because you love God and want to obey him. Therefore, God will reward your love by giving you everything you need, and you will not even have to ask him. So powerful are these first three commandments and their corresponding teachings that no further work on the tree is necessary for those who can comply with them. For everything that is needed or desired will be given to those who observe these mitzvoth without any further effort on their part. When you love God, love your neighbor, and love your enemies, God is with you. You need nothing else.

PATH 13

This path connects Kether (1) with Tiphareth (6). The teaching associated with this Path is: "You are the light of the world. A city that is established on a mountain cannot be hidden."

A person who loves God and functions under God's protection and who shares his bounties with everyone around him will be a constant source of inspiration to those who know him and a positive influence for the rest of the world. He will be like a city built on a mountain that cannot be hidden.

PATH 14

This Path connects Chokmah (2) with Binah (3). The teaching associated with it is: "If you have faith as a grain of mustard, you will ask this mountain to move and it will move and there will be nothing impossible for you."

It is difficult to love a neighbor as we love ourselves and even more difficult to love an enemy. It is as difficult as moving a mountain. But if we have faith as a grain of mustard, that is, conviction and strength of character, we can accomplish this. And once we have succeeded in such a difficult task, there is nothing we cannot accomplish. If we can do that, we can do anything. Thereafter, everything will be possible unto us.

We saw earlier, when we first discussed this teaching, that faith and lack of doubt will get us anything we want. It is more than a question of mind over matter. It is simply that being absolutely certain that something will happen "binds" that event on the material world as well as on the mental plane. It will then manifest as an actual reality.

PATH 15

This Path connects Chokmah (2) with Tiphareth (6). The teaching identified with this Path is: "Do not gather to yourself treasures on earth but in heaven."

The pleasure of overcoming and vanquishing an enemy is a very human instinct. It is the equivalent of winning a war against an evil empire from which many treasures may be gathered. But these treasures may be lost or enjoyed briefly. The rewards of loving the enemy and spreading this teaching so others may benefit from it are far greater because they will ensure we will be granted everything we truly desire.

PATH 16

This Path connects Chokmah (2) with Chesed (4). The teaching identified with it is: "If someone hits you on the right cheek, turn to him the other one."

As we saw earlier this teaching is based on the Law of Three. This law says, in fact, "Whoever does me any harm will receive in turn three times the harm he inflicted upon me. Whoever does me a good turn, will receive three times the good he bestowed upon me. Likewise, I will be punished or rewarded thrice for any evil or good I do unto others."

Loving our neighbor as we do ourselves and giving alms in secret will also be rewarded thrice in accordance with the Law of Three and this teaching of Jesus.

PATH 17

This Path connects Binah (3) and Tiphareth (6). The teaching identified with this Path is: "Be wise as serpents and gentle as doves."

The forgiveness and the love for an enemy is to be gentle as doves. To spread this teaching so that others may share in its rewards is to be wise as serpents as later those who learned that lesson may be called to forgive you should you hurt or offend them.

PATH 18

This Path connects Binah (3) with Geburah (5). The teaching identified with this Path is: "Agree quickly with your adversary lest he bring you in front of a judge and you be cast into prison."

Geburah is the sphere of judgment, where justice is dispensed. All legal matters are decided in the fifth Sephira. Jesus is telling us to agree with our adversary, to be gentle and acquiescent as a lover might be, so that our enemy will not cause our downfall. We must abstain from angry accusations and from passing hasty judgment. This self-control may result in a peaceful agreement with our adversary but it will also give us time to prepare better should we have to face a legal battle against him. Therefore the teaching is one of wise restraint rather than capitulation. This restraint and caution must always be observed in all matters connected with Geburah, where there is always the danger of violence and mayhem. Even situations that are not of a legal nature—such as undergoing a surgical procedure, which also falls under Geburah's influence—must be treated with the utmost care and caution. That is the core of this teaching.

PATH 19

This path connects Geburah (5) with Chesed (4). The teaching identified with this Path is: "If someone will not receive you or help you, shake the dust off your sandals in front of his door. It will be worse for that house than it was to Sodom and Gomorrah."

Geburah is the sphere of judgment while Chesed is the sphere of compassion, of giving. This teaching pertains to both. If someone denies you help in your time of need, that person is in fact denying the first three basic commandments of Jesus: love of God, love of the neighbor, and love of the enemy. This lack of love and compassion brings retribution in its wake, a punishment brought upon someone by the person who refuses to help. And as all divine punishments are multiplied by the Law of Three, it will be worse for that individual than it was for Sodom and Gomorrah. We saw earlier an example of how this teaching works. It is part of a divine law and no one is immune to it.

PATH 20

This Path connects Chesed (4) with Tiphareth (6). The teaching identified with this Path is: "Whoever exalts himself will be abased, and he who humbles himself will be exalted."

Chesed is the sphere associated with abundance and prosperity, and also with heads of state and people in power. Tiphareth represents riches, success, and power. People who enjoy the combined blessings of both Sephiroth are often tempted to hold themselves in high regard. Jesus warns us to avoid this temptation and to be humble in the recognition of God's blessings. Therefore we should let others sing our praises and remember that everything we have may be taken from us when we least expect it.

PATH 21

This Path connects Chesed (4) with Netzach (7). The teaching identified with this Path is: "The last will be first and the first last. For many are called but few are chosen."

This teaching is based on one of Jesus's most famous parables. In the parable he likens the kingdom of heaven to a landowner who hired some laborers in the morning to work in his vineyard for one denarius each. As the day progressed, he continued to hire more laborers. At the end of the day, he paid all his laborers one denarius each. But the ones who had been hired first felt cheated because they were paid the same wages as the ones who had started work later in the day. When they complained to the landowner, he said that he did not think the early laborers had been cheated because they had agreed to work the whole day for a denarius. As for the others, who started to work later, he paid them as he saw fit and as he could do with his money as he wished, the early laborers had no reason to complain. Therefore the last should be first and the first last.

When Jesus compares the landowner and his laborers to the kingdom of heaven, he is saying that we receive the fruit of our labors according to God's judgment. We should not complain if others have more, even when they apparently do not deserve their bounties. There may be reasons for their gain that we know nothing about. We must therefore trust God's perfect judgment in the distribution of plenty. Geburah, which represents justice, and Netzach, which represents enjoyment and pleasure, are in God's hands to bestow. What we can be sure of is that like the laborers at the vineyard, we will receive exactly what we deserve.

PATH 22

This Path connects Geburah (5) with Tiphareth (6). The teaching associated with this Path is: "Give unto Caesar what belongs to Caesar and to God what belongs to God."

This teaching is concerned with the difference between material and spiritual things. As Geburah represents justice and Tiphareth represents riches, Jesus is telling us to dispense our material wealth in a just and righteous manner, paying our debts, fulfilling our obligations, and giving everyone his due. At the same time he is telling us that by observing this moral conduct, we are also fulfilling our obligations toward God.

PATH 23

This Path connects Geburah (5) to Hod (8). The teaching identified with this Path is: "He who takes up the sword shall die by the sword."

Geburah, as we have already seen, is the sphere of war and strife. Hod is the sphere of contracts, paperwork, and business deals. Through this teaching we are told that all violent and rash actions, whether in battle or in normal everyday dealings, will have dire consequences. Contracts are not only made between potential business partners. A marriage is a contract, so is a bank loan, the lease on a house, or the foundation of a friendship. All of these valuable relationships are endangered through violent or irresponsible behavior. Therefore it is wiser to abstain from the use of force unless absolutely necessary.

PATH 24

This Path connects Tiphareth with Netzach. The teaching identified with this Path is: "You shall know a good tree by its fruit."

This teaching tells us to investigate every aspect of a situation before making an important decision concerning it. Tiphareth represents wealth, success, and power. Netzach represents love, enjoyment, and pleasure. Through this teaching Jesus is saying that we should consider every course of action carefully and know very well the circumstances surrounding every opportunity before making an actual commitment. This pertains to business matters as well as to romance and personal choices. Testing the grounds and testing the people we will be dealing with will tell us what we may expect from them. It is the equivalent of tasting the fruit of a tree. If the fruit is not sweet and rich to our taste, we will not eat it. We will simply move forward into the orchard and look for a tree that bears sweeter fruit.

PATH 25

This Path connects Tiphareth (6) with Yesod (9). The teaching identified with this Path is: "Do not worry about tomorrow, for tomorrow will bring worries of its own. Sufficient to the day is its own trouble."

Tiphareth's central influence is success and power. Yesod deals mostly with changes, transformations. In this teaching Jesus is telling us to concentrate on the moment. He is emphasizing the tremendous importance of the NOW. Nothing exists beyond the moment. We must function as if tomorrow did not exist. Our actions of today, if wise, will better our prospects for the future without having to worry about them. Our success, our attainment of power, depends on the changes and transformations we make today, NOW. That is why Jesus says that sufficient to the day is its own trouble. Whatever we do today, however insignificant in appearance, will influence tomorrow and every day thereafter.

PATH 26

This Path connects Tiphareth (6) with Hod (8). The teaching identified with this Path is: "Do not worry about what you will say. It will be given unto you at the hour in which you must speak."

This teaching is about faith and self-assurance. Whenever we have to speak with an important person, whether it is a potential employer (Tiphareth, success) or a potential spouse (Hod, contracts), it is wise not to worry about what we will say. We should be ready, know what we have to offer, and then we should relax. We must have no doubt that we will accomplish our goal and have total faith in a positive outcome. At the moment of that all-important meeting we will know exactly what to say. Words will come naturally and convincingly. Self-confidence is faith and lack of doubt.

PATH 27

This Path connects Hod (8) with Netzach (9). The teaching identified with this Path is: "No one can serve two masters. You cannot serve God and Mammon."

God represents all that is good, righteous, noble. Mammon represents evil, avarice, concupiscence. This teaching tells us that we must make a choice in our moral behavior. Whether we are dealing with business matters (Hod) or with a romantic liaison (Netzach), we must first determine our intentions. If we decide to take advantage of a trusting potential partner, we may find later on that we cannot reverse our actions. It will be difficult to convince someone who is aware of our betrayal to give us a second chance. Therefore, we must make a decision about our moral actions and stick by it. Jesus is not telling us what choice to make. He is simply telling us that once we have made a choice we must stand by it.

PATH 28

This Path connects Netzach (7) with Yesod (9). The teaching associated with this Path is: "Beware of false prophets."

Yesod, as we have seen, is the sphere of illusions. Netzach deals with love, pleasures, and enjoyment. A false prophet is anyone who makes promises that he does not intend to keep. Therefore we should be careful not to believe everything we hear or depend on promises without foundation (Yesod) in the illusory hope that they will bring us love or pleasures (Netzach).

PATH 29

This Path connects Netzach (7) with Malkuth (10). The teaching identified with this Path is: "Unless you be like little children, you will not enter the kingdom of heaven."

Children have trust and faith. They have no doubt that their parents will always love and protect them. This love is their enjoyment and their pleasure (Netzach). Malkuth is the kingdom of heaven. It represents stability and security. We can only achieve these things if we have trust and faith in the love of God, our Father.

PATH 30

This Path connects Hod (8) with Yesod (9). The teaching associated with this Path is: "If a blind man leads another blind man they will both fall by the wayside."

This teaching tells us to beware of making any business deals (Hod) with someone equally or less experienced than we are. Such a business will have a false foundation (Yesod) and can only lead to disaster. This also applies to any relationship where both persons are inexperienced in the ways of life.

PATH 31

This Path connects Hod (8) to Malkuth (10). The teaching identified with this Path is: "By your words you shall be justified and by your words you shall be condemned."

Jesus is telling us here to be careful in the way we express ourselves, lest our words or our intentions be misinterpreted. This applies equally to personal or business relationships (Hod), as any misunderstanding will affect our lives (Malkuth). On the other hand, a clear understanding between ourselves and others can only lead to success in our relationships.

PATH 32

This Path connects Yesod (9) with Malkuth (10). The teaching identified with this Path is: "Whoever hears these sayings of mine and does them, I will liken him to a wise man who built his house on the rock. And the rain descended, the floods came and the winds blew and beat on that house and it did not fall, for it was founded on the rock."

This was Jesus's last teaching during the Sermon on the Mount. Path 32, linking Yesod and Malkuth, is the most important of all the Paths because it marks the ascension from the world of matter (Malkuth) to the world of mind and spirit (Yesod). When Jesus compares his teachings to a house built on a rock, he is referring to a spiritual foundation, symbolized by Yesod. Whoever follows his teachings will be able to withstand all the trials of life (Malkuth) and will survive all the temptations and illusions of Yesod. These teachings, founded on the rock of faith and absence of doubt, are the keys of the kingdom.

So far we have been discussing the thirty-two Paths of the Tree of Life in the light of thirty-two of Jesus's teachings. These teachings are the core of Jesus' commandments or mitzvoth. However, there is one teaching of Jesus where all of his commandments are epitomized. This teaching was also part of the Sermon on the Mount. Speaking to the multitudes who had gathered to listen to him, Jesus said, "Therefore, do unto others as you would have them do unto you, for this is the Law and the prophets."

This saying of Jesus, known as the Golden Rule, summarizes everything he taught. It also embodies the Ten Commandments and the ten Sephiroth of the Tree of Life. That is why Jesus says that this teaching is the Law, that is, the Torah, upon which are based all the works of the prophets.

The keys of the kingdom given by Jesus as the core of his teachings will be a useful tool for those who apply them to their daily life in conjunction with the Sephiroth and the Paths of the Tree of Life. Seen in this light, they are the greatest body of teachings of a moral and social order that have ever been given to humanity. This was Jesus's divine mission, an illuminating plethora of wisdom that transcends his condition as a man and a teacher. His cosmic message and its spiraling repercussions throughout the centuries are what mark him as a divine messenger, a gift of God to Israel and to the world, a true Messiah.

13

REVELATIONS

He went teaching daily in the
temple. But the chief priests
and the scribes . . . were
seeking to destroy him.

—LUKE 47

I t is clear from the various gospels that Jesus taught in the temple. He could not have done this if he had not been an accredited rabbi. All rabbis in good standing had to have established, well-known families and had to be married. Clearly, Jesus must have satisfied these criteria; otherwise he would not have been allowed to teach in the temple, and he did this on a daily basis. Why, then, did the chief priests and scribes seek to destroy Jesus? We have a direct clue in Mark 61–63:

> Again the high priest began to question him and said to him: "Are you the Christ, the son of the Blessed One?" Then Jesus said: "I am and you will see the son of man sitting at the right hand of power and coming with the clouds of heaven." At this, the high priest tore his inner garments and said: "What further need do we have of witnesses? You heard the blasphemy."

To the high priest of the temple, Jesus's assertion that he was indeed the Messiah was a blasphemy punishable by death. But long before Jesus spoke those words, the priests and scribes were seeking to destroy him. His admission that he was the long-awaited deliverer of Israel simply signed his death sentence.

As we have already seen, Jesus's name in Aramaic was Yeheshua/ Yehoshuah, which means "God delivers." In his introduction to his

translation of the Sepher Yetzirah, renowned Hebrew scholar and kabbalist Aryeh Kaplan mentions a leading sage of the first century called
Rabbi Yehoshuah (ben Chanayna) (see Kaplan, *Sepher Yetzirah*). Ben
Chanayna means son of Chanayna, but in those early times such a sur-
name may have been added for further identification. This teacher
lived around the same time as Jesus and in the same area. It is entirely
possible that Rabbi Yehoshuah and Jesus were one and the same man.
It would certainly seem extremely coincidental that two well-known
teachers of the same name should have lived near Jerusalem at the
same time.

Rabbi Yehoshuah was a renowned kabbalist and one of the five leading disciples of Rabbi Yohannan ben Zakkai (47 BCE–73 CE), acknowledged leader of the Jews after the destruction of the temple. Rabbi
Yehoshuah was Rabbi Yochanan's main disciple in the mysteries of the
kabbalistic Merkaba (Holy Chariot), and eventually became known as
the greatest expert of his time in the occult. According to tradition,
Rabbi Yehoshuah is credited with the statement that he could take
squashes and pumpkins and turn them into beautiful trees that could
produce other beautiful trees.

The mystical significance of crowns *(tagin)* on Hebrew letters was
handed down from rabbi to rabbi in the following manner: Menachem
revealed the mysteries to Rabbi Nehunia, who passed it on to Rabbi
Elazar, who passed it on to Rabbi Yehoshuah, who passed it on to
Rabbi Akiba.

Menachem served as vice president of the Sanhedrin, Supreme
Council of the Jews, under Hillel, who is said to have lived circa 70 BCE
–10 CE. Hillel was the first Jewish scholar to systematize the interpretation of scriptural law. Hillel's emphasis on adherence to ethical
norms, personal piety, humility, and loving concern for one's neighbors
anticipated the moral teachings of Jesus, who may have studied under
him.

Many religious authorities identify Menachem with Menachem the
Essene, who is mentioned in the works of Josephus (see Josephus,

Works). When Herod was a child, Menachem prophesied that Herod would be king one day. Later on, when Herod ascended the throne of Israel, he honored Menachem and the other Essenes. For this reason, Menachem could no longer maintain his position as vice president of the Sanhedrin and resigned his position.

If we accept this tradition, the Essenes were conversant with the mystical arts and taught them to some of the Talmudic masters, such as Rabbi Nehunia, from whom they would eventually pass on to Rabbi Yehoshuah. Josephus states that the Essenes used the names of angels in their rituals and were able to foretell the future, using various purifications and the methods of the ancient prophets.

As we have seen, Rabbi Yehoshuah passed on the mysteries of the crowns on the letters to Rabbi Akiba. He also revealed to Rabbi Akiba the mysteries of the Merkabah, one of the central teachings of the Kabbalah, as well as other important occult lore. Rabbi Akiba was the teacher of Rabbi Simeon ben Jochai, who revealed to the world the mysteries of the Kabbalah in the Zohar, the most important of the kabbalistic books.

It is clear from the preceding that Rabbi Yehoshuah, who was the teacher of Rabbi Akiba, who in turn was the teacher of Rabbi Simeon ben Jochai, is the ultimate source of the Kabbalah, according to tradition.

The Talmudic tradition teaches that the general seat of kabbalistic teaching in the first century was the town of Emmaus, where both Rabbi Nehunia and Rabbi Elazar lived. As we saw earlier, Rabbi Elazar was one of Rabbi Yehoshuah's teachers who passed on to him the mysteries of the crowns on the Hebrew letters.

In Luke 24:13–20, the evangelist tells us what took place on the third day after the crucifixion:

> But look on that very day two of them (the disciples) were journeying to a village about seven miles distant from Jerusalem and named Emmaus . . . As they were conversing and discussing, Jesus himself approached and began walking

with them . . . and they (spoke) to him . . . "Concerning Jesus the Nazarene, who became a prophet powerful in work and word before God and all the people; and how our chief priests and rulers handed him over to the sentence of death and impaled him. But we were hoping that this man was the one destined to deliver Israel . . ."

What is important in this biblical passage is that after the crucifixion two of the disciples were traveling to Emmaus, the kabbalistic center of the time, and that Jesus joined them. Furthermore, they told Jesus, whom they had not recognized, that Jesus had become a "prophet powerful in work and word before God and the people."

From this we can see that Jesus and his disciples knew Emmaus and must have also known what was taught there. It is also clear that Jesus —Rabbi Yehoshuah—had become a powerful and renowned prophet. But Rabbi Yehoshuah fell from grace in the eyes of the Sanhedrin and the chief priests. Why? Because he chose to reveal to the masses things which were meant only for the elect and which passed from the mouth of the teacher to the ear of the disciple in the time-honored tradition of Israel. That is why the chief priests and the scribes sought to destroy him.

Rabbi Yehoshuah did these things because he believed himself to be the Messiah, the deliverer of Israel, and as such he was concerned with the salvation of all the people, not just a precious few. He sought to instruct them in the mysteries of the Kabbalah, which he did through parables and sermons, thinly veiled, but still clear to those "who had ears to listen." This incurred the wrath of the Sanhedrin and the chief priests and scribes. Those revelations were the reason Jesus was condemned to die. His assertion that he was the Messiah gave the chief priests a powerful reason to sign a death warrant. But they had already decided Jesus's fate before he proclaimed himself as the Messiah.

Through the revelations of the Talmudic tradition, we know of the existence of Rabbi Yehoshuah, a leading sage of the first century, who was the source of the Kabbalah as we know it today. Rabbi Yehoshuah—

Jesus Christ—taught the world the supreme cosmological principles of the Kabbalah in simple words accessible to all humanity: words like love, trust, will, faith, compassion, justice, beauty, glory, wisdom, and understanding, easily identified with the spheres of the kabbalistic Tree of Life. And if Jesus Christ was the source of the Kabbalah, then the Kabbalah is Christian, where Christian means messianic.

RITUALS & MEDITATIONS

THE IMPORTANCE
OF RITUAL

A ritual may be described as a ceremony central to an act of worship or as a repeated act that establishes ordinary modes of conduct. Getting up every morning and going through the familiar routine of washing up, getting dressed, and having breakfast before going to work is a form of ritual. We do it almost automatically and it helps bring stability and normalcy to our everyday lives. Every human existence is made of many such rituals. In the United States, Christmas, New Year, Thanksgiving, and Halloween are rituals we observe as a matter of fact every year. Jews observe Hannukah, Yom Kippur, and Rosh Hashanah, and other cultures around the world observe similar rites with equal regularity. There are also the rites of passage such as baptisms, weddings, and bar mitzvahs. Religious ceremonies, such as the consecration of bread and wine in the Christian Eucharist, are also rituals. Therefore we can say that our entire lives are surrounded by rituals. It is an intrinsic part of our mental, emotional, and spiritual makeup.

Religious or magical rituals are intended to establish a link between ourselves and the creative force of the universe. In Kabbalah, rituals are of paramount importance. They are mostly based on the Tree of Life, but some seek to contact the Godhead in other ways. It is important to understand that the forces symbolized by the various spheres of the Tree of Life are not alien, supernatural entities residing in a mystical, ethereal realm. Rather they are a very real part of the human psyche, what Jung called the collective unconscious. The various aspects of God, the archangels, and angelic choirs associated with each Sephira may be identified as archetypes of the collective unconscious. According to Jung, an archetype is an autonomous complex within the human personality. As such, it functions independently from the conscious personality and "behaves" as if it were a separate entity. Each archetype controls a different aspect of the human personality and/or a different human endeavor. For the perfect balance of the personality, and therefore for mental health, it is vital that each archetype be well developed and assimilated by the individual. When one archetype is allowed to overpower the rest of the personality, as in the case of Nietszche's Zarathustra, the result can be a mental disturbance or dissociation of the personality—a leading symptom of psychosis.

There are many archetypes. Among them Jung identified the Persona or conscious personality, the face we present to the outside word; the Shadow, which is the concentration of all negative tendencies in a human being; and the Self, which encompasses the most exalted principles in each individual (see Jung, *Archetypes*). The Self may be identified with the Atman, the Holy Guardian Angel, the god within. There is a continuous struggle between the archetypes, each vying for control of the personality. Each evil or negative act is the result of the Shadow's influence. Likewise, every noble or generous action is influenced by the power of the Self. When the archetypes are finally balanced and in perfect harmony, it is said that the person has accomplished what Jung called the individuation process. At this moment, all the archetypes revolve around the Self and the conscious personality has perfect control of the individual's life.

Jung found evidence for the universal archetypes in the similarity of symbolism in myths, religions, fairy tales, sagas, and even poetry. Among them he cited the archetype of the eternal cosmic child as in Jesus, the infant Hermes, Zeus, or Moses. Also of great importance is the archetype of the universal creative mother, identified with Nature, the female principle, and with the great goddesses of the world's religions. Finally, he also identified the God archetype, which varies in accordance with the various religions of the world and with each individual's cultural and sociological situation.

To Jung, the God archetype was of great importance. He believed that an individual whose deep psychic images impel him to be the instrument of such a transcendental archetype has available to him a power far greater than his own individuality could supply. God—or the God archetype—is considered to be the source of personal fortune, punishment, inspiration, health and sickness, and the meaning of life. This was the view of the Western world in its beginnings, but it is not true today. It was true in ancient times and in the Middle Ages, but not in our modern times. The fast pace of our modern technologies has driven the God archetype underground. It has been replaced by the modern human being's pursuit of "truth." In consequence of this, the vast energies attached to the God archetype are released into the human psyche and since it is too small to contain it, the result is chaos and confusion. The image of man has taken the place of the image of God.

In those societies where the God archetype has been strong, God and Truth have tended to merge and identify with each other. Such was the case with the writers of the Old and New Testament. But in our modern societies, where the God archetype has lost its force, God and Truth have become separate. The archetype of Truth displays its own individuality. We find ourselves speaking in terms of logic, science, intellect, and reason. These are humanity's gods now. We are even beginning to set our own criteria for judging the truth of God's existence. The subject matter of Truth is material things. But the Truth archetype retains, despite its close relation with matter, vestiges of its earlier identification with the God archetype. For that reason, the search for scientific knowledge is regarded by some as the highest good and the highest truth. It is even regarded, as in the case of Einstein, as the equivalent of knowing God himself. But all our rational thoughts and scientific calculations are impelled by forces that are beyond the reach of rationality. Physical equations are the work of consciousness, but the faith in physics and its related sciences and technologies are not the result of rational choices. They are not questions of intellect but rather involve unconscious commitments with a deep religious undercurrent.

The power motivating our modern, materialistic ideologies has a dual source. On the one hand, it comes from the energy inherent in the archetypal symbols that express the transcendence of matter and the image of truth; and on the other hand, it comes from the vast sums of psychic energy which have been released by the "death" of God in the modern psyche. These uncontrolled and uncontrollable energies have caused an inflation of the human ego, expressing the worship of our intellectual capacities. Out of this unrealistic view of our mental powers may come the first indications of the self-destruction of Western civilization. Jung cites the case of Nietszche as a dynamic parallel with the abandonment of the God archetype in our modern times. Nietszche was an atheist who announced the death of God triumphantly (see Nietszche, *Thus Spake Zarathustra*). But the "death" of the God archetype resulted in Nietszche himself taking the place of God. When this happens in an individual's personality, the inflatory effect is so great that the ego is bound to be disintegrated, as it did in Nietszche. When its equivalent takes place on a larger scale, such as the generality of humanity, the psychic patterns and results are bound to be the same. Up to this point, the parallel holds, and it seems to be only a matter of time before the psychic "inflation" of Western civilization will bring about its own collapse.

Paradoxically, the "death" of the God archetype in modern societies opens the possibility of a new relationship with God based on an eventual richer understanding of what God means. There is the distinct hope of a renascence of the God archetype based on a complete reversal in the traditional Western orientation toward religious life. This reversal would entail a more sensitive approach to events taking place in the depths of the Self and a larger understanding of our psychic structure. This will draw increasing numbers of people into the very center of their beings, where God can eventually be reborn.

Lastly to be considered is Jung's concept of the Principle of Opposites. Love and hate, heat and cold, darkness and light—are all opposites in continuous tension. This tension releases vast amounts of what Jung called psychic energies or libido. The amount of energy generated and set loose varies with the intensity of the internal conflict within the individual. The greater the tension, the greater the energy released. Jung found evidence of these opposites, as with the archetypes, in the world's religions and mythologies, sagas and fairy tales. The Chinese concept of the Ying-Yang and the Sephira of the left and right hand of the Tree of Life were seen by Jung as examples of these opposites. They must always be in perfect balance for the energy released by the deep unconscious to be controlled by the conscious personality.

This brings us to the importance of ritual. During a ritual, large amounts of psychic energies are released from the deep unconscious. These energies are archetypal in nature and are channeled by the individual through the help of the archetype being contacted. The energies or libido are manifested, that is, realized in the material world as actual events. In a kabbalistic ritual based on the Tree of Life, for example, the principle of opposites comes into effect. The Sephiroth on opposite sides of the tree are concentrated on, thereby creating a tension between them, which in turn releases large amounts of psychic energies. These energies are manifested in the material world, depending on the things "ruled" by those Sephiroth. If the result intended is abundance and prosperity, the Sephira chosen for meditation should be the fourth, Chesed, which rules those things. Its opposite is Geburah, and it must also be meditated upon in order to balance their energies. If the Sephira chosen lies within the Middle Pillar, it requires no other Sephira for balance as it has within itself the harmonious contents of the entire tree.

The names of God and the angels associated with each sphere are all archetypes and are the keys that unlock the energies necessary for the success of the ritual.

Every ritual, kabbalistic or otherwise, may be explained along these Jungian concepts and they all function within the depths of the unconscious through the inner workings of the archetypes. This is the rationale of the ritual and its importance in human life.

The following pages list a series of rituals, some simple and others more complex, but all of which work with one or more archetypes.

THE RITUAL OF
THE NEW MOON

My father, who was a fine biblical scholar, taught me this ritual many years ago. He always said that it was important to study the scriptures carefully because there was much hidden between the lines, and that even though much had been lost in the translations, enough remained to be learned by the conscientious scholar. This is also the purpose behind the Talmud and the Midrash, which provide innumerable ways to interpret the scriptures.

According to the tradition behind this ritual, God descends upon Earth for exactly five minutes at the time of the New Moon. The fact that there are different time zones throughout the planet makes no difference, as the spirit of God is linked directly with the New Moon itself at this moment.

What is necessary for the success of the ritual is that it be conducted exactly at the start of the New Moon in the time zone where the person resides. This necessitates the use of a reliable astrological calendar or an ephemeris for the place. Both give the exact time of the start of the New Moon month by month.

Once the time has been ascertained, the person prepares beforehand by washing carefully and dressing in white. He then lights two white candles and reads Psalm 81, beginning the reading at exactly the time of the New Moon. He asks God's blessing and makes one single wish, which must be just and not impinge upon anyone else's will or cause harm to anyone. All of this must be done within five minutes. If he is careful to observe these simple rules, his wish will be granted. This can be repeated every month with a different wish each time.

This simple ritual is very effective and extraordinary things may be accomplished through its use, if it is conducted with faith and reverence.

After the ritual, a small glass of sweet white wine should be drunk. Thanks should be given to God for his blessing. The candles are extinguished and reused in the next ritual.

LUNAR BLESSING

This ritual is found in the Me'am Lo'ez, one of the most famous works of the Kabbalah, hailed as the outstanding work of Ladino literature— Ladino being, of course, the Spanish Kabbalah. It has the same status as the Talmud and the Mishnah among Eastern Jews. It was written in 1730 by Rabbi Jakov Kuli, one of the greatest Sephardic sages of his time. The book was translated into English by renowned kabbalist Rabbi Aryeh Kaplan.

According to an ancient Jewish tradition, the Moon is not like any other celestial body, as it is renewed each month. For that reason each time there is a New Moon, God must be thanked for this wonder. According to the Me'am Lo'ez, seeing the New Moon is like welcoming the divine presence. The great sense of awe that the ancient Jews felt for the New Moon is the reason why they devised a lunar, instead of a solar calendar. All major Jewish holidays always fall around the New Moon, especially New Year. Every New Moon is celebrated by chanting the Hallel, which is a collection of psalms and other sacred writings. *Hallel* means "praises." The well-known *Hallelujah* means "Praises unto God": Hallel-u-Jah. Jah is one of God's most sacred names.

The blessing must be said after the *molad*, that is, when the New Moon first becomes visible in the sky. Some scholars say the blessing should be said immediately after the molad. Others believe the best time is three days after the molad, while still others say one should wait until seven days after the molad. The latter is the generally accepted time.

The preferred day for the lunar blessing is on a Saturday, as it is the Sabbath day. The Moon must not be covered by clouds. If the sky is cloudy and the blessing cannot be said on a Saturday, it is believed that it is a sign that the month will not be successful.

If the blessing cannot be said on a Saturday because of inclement weather, it may be said during the rest of the week, except Fridays. The blessing can be said until the Full Moon, but never afterwards, as it is then considered a vain blessing. Any month when the blessing is not said because of cloudy skies is considered an evil portent.

The lunar blessing must not be undertaken lightly, and once the practice begins it should be continued as long as the person lives.

The blessing should be done in the open, but if this is not possible, it may be done indoors, as long as the Moon may be seen through a window.

The person conducting this ritual must be clean, dressed nicely, preferably in white, and must not be barefoot. He should not stare at the Moon. He should glance at it briefly and lower his eyes. His feet should be placed together. He then says:

"Praise God! Praise God from heaven, praise him in the heights. Praise him all his angels, praise him all his host. Praise him Sun and Moon, praise him all you stars of light. Praise him O heaven of the heavens, and the waters above the heavens. They will praise the name of God, for he commanded and they were created. He established them forever, a rule given that is not violated.

"Blessed are you, O God our Lord, King of the Universe, who created the heavens with his word, and with the breath of his mouth all his host. He gave them a decree and a time, that they not change their appointed task. They rejoice and are glad to do the will of their masters. He is a true worker, whose works are truth. And to the Moon he said that it should be renewed, a crown of beauty for the ones carried from the womb, which, in the future, will be renewed (like the Moon) to thank their creator because of the glory of his kingdom. Blessed are you, O God, renewer of the months."

The person then says three times:

"May there be a good sign for us and for all Israel.

"Blessed be your former, blessed be your maker, blessed be your creator."

The person then lifts himself upon his toes and says three times:

"Just as we lift ourselves up toward you, O Moon, and cannot touch you, so if others reach out to us, let them not be able to touch us to do evil. May they never have power over us.

"Fear and terror befell them, through greatness of your arm they were silent like stone. Stone like silent were they arm your of greatness through them befell terror and fear (Exodus 15:16).

"David, King of Israel, living and enduring. Amen, Amen, Amen. Forever, Forever, Forever.

"A pure heart create for me O God, and a proper spirit renew within me" (Psalm 51:12).

The following is said only once:

"It is the sound of my Lover. Behold He comes, skipping on the mountains, bounding on the hills. My Lover is like a gazelle, like a young hart. Behold he stands behind our wall, overseeing from the windows, peering through the cracks (Song of Songs 2:8, 9).

"A song of steps: I lift my eyes to the mountains, from where shall come my help? My help is from God, Maker of heaven and earth. He will not let your foot slip; your Watcher slumbers not. Behold the Guardian of Israel does not slumber. He does not sleep. God is your Bodyguard. God is your Shadow, by your right side. By the day the Sun will not strike you, nor the Moon by night. God will safeguard you from all evil. He will safeguard your soul. God will safeguard your going out and your coming in, now and forever (Psalm 121).

"Praise God! Praise the Omnipotent in his holy place. Praise him in the firmament of his might. Praise him in his strength. Praise him for his immense greatness. Praise him with the sound of the shofar. Praise him with harp and lute. Praise him with drum and dance. Praise him with strings and flute. Praise him with loud cymbals. Every soul, praise God! Praise God! (Psalm 150)

"Who is this coming from the desert, leaning on her beloved? (Song of Songs 8:5)

"To him who grants victory through melodies, a psalm, a song: May God be gracious to us and bless us; may he makes his face shine on us—Selah. That Your way be known in the earth, Your salvation among all nations. Let peoples all thank you, O God, let peoples all thank you. Let nations rejoice and sing, for You will judge peoples fairly, and You will lead nations on earth—Selah. Let peoples thank you O God, let peoples all thank you. The earth has yielded its crops. May God, our God, bless us. May God bless us and let all the ends of the earth fear him" (Psalm 67).

The person then finishes the blessing with these words:

"The school of Rabbi Ishmael taught: If Israel would only be worthy to greet their heavenly Father once a month, it would be sufficient. Abaya said: The lunar blessing must therefore be said while standing."

It is customary to shake one's clothes after finishing the blessing and say: "Peace to you, peace to you" (Shalom Alekhem, Shalom Alekhem).

SOLAR BLESSING

A commentary should be inserted here about the solar blessing. According to the Me'am Lo'ez, every twenty-eight years the Sun completes a cycle and returns to the precise place in the sky where it was on the fourth day of creation when, according to Genesis, the Sun and the Moon were created. This happens in the beginning of spring (Tekufah Nissan) on a Wednesday morning. The blessing should be said at sunrise. The words are simple:

"Blessed are you, O God our Lord, King of the Universe, Maker of the work of creation."

The last time the solar blessing was said was 1981. It will be said again in 2009. Anyone can say it as long as the sky is clear and the Sun may be seen arising on the horizon. It is a date to remember.

NECTAR OF LEVANAH

Levanah is the Hebrew word for the Moon. The sphere of Yesod is associated with the Moon. For that reason, the Moon is seen as a source of great spiritual energy. The Nectar of Levanah is a special drink prepared during the New and the Full Moon. It is made by mixing heavy cream or half and half with white wine, sugar, and a beaten egg white. The mixture is poured into a blue wine glass or a silver chalice. If possible, a moonstone should be placed inside the liquid. A silver candle is then lit in front of the wine glass. This offer is made in the name of the Shekinah and the archangel Gabriel, who rules the sphere of Yesod. The candle is allowed to burn for an hour. It is then extinguished in the liquid, which is drunk in one single draught. This simple ritual should be done at night on both the New and the Full Moon. It is an enriching spiritual experience and provides great positive energies during the lunar month.

NECTAR OF SHEMESH

Shemesh is the name of the Sun in Hebrew. As the Nectar of Levanah is prepared for the New and Full Moons to acquire lunar energies, the Nectar of Shemesh is prepared once a month to acquire solar energies. The specific date when the nectar is made coincides with the day when the Sun enters a new zodiac sign. Following are the twelve signs and the dates when they begin:

Aries—March 20	Libra—September 22
Taurus—April 20	Scorpio—October 23
Gemini—May 21	Sagittarius—November 22
Cancer—June 21	Capricorn—December 21
Leo—July 22	Aquarius—January 20
Virgo—August 22	Pisces—February 18

The Nectar of Shemesh is prepared on each of the preceding dates to gather the solar energies that arise with their respective signs at that time.

The nectar is made by beating the yolk of an egg until it is pale yellow. White wine, cream, and sugar are added. The liquid is then poured into a yellow or golden goblet, and if possible a sunstone, a citrine, or a piece of amber should be placed inside it. A yellow or golden candle is lit for an hour while the person meditates on the significance of the day and asks mentally that the solar energies of that particular sign be concentrated in the liquid. An hour later the candle is extinguished in the liquid, which is drunk by the person. This ritual must be done during the daytime and falls under the aegis of the sixth Sephira, Tiphareth. The names of God and the presiding archangel of the sphere are Jehovah elo ve Daath and Raphael, respectively. The names must be concentrated upon as the liquid is drunk.

THE RITUAL OF FORGIVENESS

There are three important rituals that are conducted when a person decides to identify with God and place himself under the Creator's divine mercies. These are the ritual of forgiveness, the ritual of renunciation and the ritual of ascension. The first and most important of these rituals is the ritual of forgiveness when the person forgives those who have offended or hurt him and asks God's forgiveness in return. This ritual is ruled by the sixth sphere, Tiphareth, which is the Sephira of total forgiveness. It should be conducted on a Sunday and the Moon should be waxing. The names of God and the ruling archangel are Jehovah elo ve Daath and Raphael, respectively.

The person conducting the ritual should begin by writing the names of the people who offended him on a piece of unlined white paper. Next to each name he should write the offense.

Before conducting any ritual, the room where it will take place must be cleansed of negative or destructive energies. This may be done by sprinkling salt water around the place. Salt is considered to be the purest of all minerals and a deterrent of negative forces. That is why salt is used by the priest during the ceremony of baptism. It is also helpful to burn some incense.

Once the room has been cleansed, the person should visualize a circle of white light surrounding the area. Mental projections are very powerful and although the light will not be visible to the naked eye, it will be present in the mental spheres.

The person should be dressed in white and barefoot. He should face the east where the Sun rises every morning. The east is the preferred location of most magical and kabbalistic rituals as positive forces are said to rise with the Sun. Traditionally, rituals of black magic are conducted in the west because that is the place where the Sun sets and the dark forces reside.

After the circle of light has been visualized, the person places a deep metal container on the floor. Any type of container will do as long as it is fireproof. Inside the container are placed several pieces of charcoal which are then lit. Facing the metal container should be placed a golden candle holder with a white taper, also lit. Over the pieces of charcoal are then sprinkled several laurel leaves (sacred to the Sun since ancient times), a small piece of camphor (sacred to the Moon), and myrrh and frankincense (traditional offerings to God). As the smoke rises from the burning charcoals, the person reads the names written on the paper and says:

"In the holy name of Jehovah elo ve Daath, God manifested in the sphere of the Sun, and the great archangel Raphael, I forgive these persons all the harm they may have caused me and I release them into the light. Likewise, I ask my Creator's forgiveness for all my human errors and his blessings during the entire course of my life. May it be so. Amen."

He then burns the paper in the light of the taper and places it over the burning incense.

This is the end of the ritual. The taper is extinguished without blowing upon it and the incense is allowed to burn itself out. The remnants, including the paper's ashes, are then disposed of.

RITUAL OF RENUNCIATION

This ritual was designed with the intention of returning a person's will to God and placing his entire life in the Creator's hands. It is done only after the Ritual of Forgiveness. The ritual is conducted on a Thursday as this is the day ruled by the sphere of Chesed, where prosperity and human success are to be found. The Moon should be waxing.

The person conducting the ritual should be clean, dressed in white and barefoot. He should be facing the east. The same metal container and the white taper used in the ritual of forgiveness should be used. As in the previous ritual, the place should be cleansed with salt water and a circle of white light should be visualized surrounding the area.

Several pieces of charcoal are placed inside the container and lit. Frankincense, myrrh, a bit of camphor and hyssop are sprinkled over the coals. The white taper is lit. The person then says:

"In the holy name of El, the name of the Creator in the Sephira of Chesed, and the great archangel Sadkiel, who rules it and all human endeavors and success, and in the holy name of Elohim Gebor, the name of the Creator in the opposite Sephira, Geburah, and the great Archangel Kamael, who rules it, I surrender unto the Creator my will and renounce all my human aspirations. I place my destiny and my life in his divine hands in complete trust and reverence, knowing that he will lead me in the perfect path of enlightenment and attainment. I know all my human needs will be met and I will have peace, joy, love, and prosperity all my days. May it be so. Amen."

The paper where these words are written is then burned in the taper's flame and placed upon the burning coals. This is the end of the ritual.

RITUAL OF ASCENSION

This ritual is done after the rituals of forgiveness and renunciation. It must be done on a Sunday and the Moon should be waxing. As in the first two rituals, the room must be cleansed with salt water and a circle of light visualized around the area. The person conducting the ritual should be clean, dressed in white and barefoot. He should face the east. Frankincense and myrrh should be placed over burning charcoals in the same metal container.

On the floor, facing the east, the person places ten small candle holders in the form of the Tree of Life. A different color candle is placed in each of the candle holders. A white candle is placed on the candle holder representing the first Sephira, Malkuth; a grey candle on the candle holder representing the second, Chokmah; a black candle on the third, Binah; a blue candle on the fourth, Chesed; a red candle on the fifth, Geburah; a yellow candle on the sixth, Tiphareth; a green candle on the seventh, Netzach; an orange candle on the eighth, Hod; a violet candle on the ninth, Yesod; and a brown candle on the tenth, Malkuth.

The person lights the brown candle and says:

"This is the light of Malkuth, the sphere of the Earth, the inferior world, the microcosm, where my mortal body resides. In the name of Adonai ha Aretz, the manifestation of the Creator in this Sephira, and the great archangel Sandalphon, who rules it, my spirit ascends through the spheres of the Middle Pillar toward the sphere of Kether, the ultimate light of the macrocosm who is the soul of the universe. Through this ascension I leave behind all my worldly cares, represented by the spheres of the left and right hand of the tree, and seek to unite with God."

The violet candle is then lit and the person says:

"This is the light of Yesod, the sphere of the Moon, where all dreams and imaginings are nurtured and where all that is to be is first visualized. In the name of Shaddai el Chai, the name of the Creator manifested in this Sephira, and the great archangel Gabriel, who rules it, my spirit ascends to the sphere of Yesod, leaving behind the world of matter that is Malkuth, in my search for the divine cosmic light."

The person pauses for a few moments, visualizing that he stands on the center of the Moon, a vast globe of silver light surrounded by violet and purple hues. When he feels himself saturated with silver light, he lights the yellow candle and says:

"This is the light of Tiphareth, the sphere of the Sun, giver of life, the midway point between darkness and light, the human and the divine. Here is forgiveness and love, beauty and redemption, the light of the crucified Christ. Here the spirit soars to the cosmic point which is the Ain Soph and dwells among the angels. In the name of Jehovah elo ve Daath, the manifestation of the Creator in this sphere, and the great archangel Raphael, who rules it, my spirit ascends to the sphere of

Tiphareth, leaving behind the sphere of Yesod, the world of the mind, in my quest for the world of the spirit."

The person pauses again and visualizes that he is in the center of the Sun, in the midst of a blinding radiance, where everything disappears in the bright amber light. Very slowly, he feels he is blending with the Sun's life-giving light until he is one with it. For a few moments, all human thoughts disappear and are replaced by an indescribable sense of total love and peace.

At this point, the white candle is lit and the person says:

"This is the eternal flame of Kether, the point of light of the Ain Soph. This is the place where my spirit was born and the cosmos came into being. This is the grace of God, the Almighty Creator, where universes take form and the atom splits into thunder and lightning. This is the place of the All and the No-Thing. This is the true reality of being. In the name of Eheieh, the supreme manifestation of the Creator in the sphere of Kether, and the great archangel Metraton, who rules it, my spirit ascends to the sphere of the All and becomes one with the Supernal Light."

At this moment the person feels his very being absorbed by the divine light and his consciousness blends with the soul of the universe. He remains in this state as long as he needs to feel the full power of the experience.

This is a very transcendental ritual and if conducted with faith and reverence, it will transform the person's life. Life will be easier and nothing will disturb his peace of mind.

After the end of the ritual, the candles are extinguished and everything is cleared away.

These three rituals are clearly not for everyone, but those who decide to do them will find their lives enriched in myriad ways. They are among the most exalted of all the kabbalistic rituals.

APPENDIX
The Sephiroth of the Tree of Life

SEPHIRA I
KETHER

Title: The Crown

Description: The Vast Countenance, Arik Anpin; the Primordial Point, Macrosopos; the Head that Is Not; Ancient of Days; Concealed of the Concealed; Existence of Existences

Associated Keywords: Unity, union, pure consciousness, the Godhead, manifestation, beginning, source, emanation

Spiritual Experience: Union with God

Path: First Path of Wisdom: the Admirable Intelligence; the Supreme Crown

Virtue: Attainment

Vice: None

God Name: AHIH, Eheieh

Archangel: Metraton, angel of the Presence, he who brings others to the face of God

Angelic Order: Chaioth ha Qadesh, the Holy Living Creatures

Image: Bearded king in profile

Planet: First Swirlings (Rashith ha Gilgalim), also Neptune

Element: Root of Air

Colors:

    Atziluth—brilliance

    Briah—white brilliance

    Yetzirah—white brilliance

    Assiah—white flecked with gold

Physical Body: Cranium

Symbols: Point, swastika

Plant: Almond flower

Animal: None

Incense: Ambergris

Metal: None

Stone: Diamond

Human Focus: Growth

Correspondences in Other Pantheons:

    Egyptian—Osiris

    Greek—Aither

    Roman—Aether

    Scandinavian—Ymir

    Hindu—Brahman

SEPHIRA 2
CHOKMAH

Title: Wisdom

Description: Aba (the father), seed of creation, discernment, masculine active potency, the Supernal Father, the original flash of intuition

Associated Keywords: Pure creative energy, life force, universal truth

Spiritual Experience: Vision of God

Path: Second Path of Wisdom, the Illuminating Intelligence, the splendor of the Supreme Unity

Virtue: Devotion

Vice: None

God Name: IHVH, Jehovah

Archangel: Ratziel, the Herald of the Deity, the Prince of Princes of the knowledge of concealed things

Angelic Order: Ophanim, Wheels, Cherubim

Image: Bearded male

Planet: Mazlot, Zodiac, Uranus

Element: Root of Fire

Colors:

    Atziluth—light blue

    Briah—grey

    Yetzirah—iridescent grey

    Assiah—white flecked with red, blue, yellow

Physical Body: Left side of face

Symbols: Phallus, straight line

Plant: Amaranth

Animal: Man

Incense: Musk

Metal: None

Stone: Ruby, turquoise

Human Focus: None

Correspondences in Other Pantheons:

Egyptian—Thoth

Greek—Uranus

Roman—Coelus

Scandinavian—Odin

Hindu—Vishnu

SEPHIRA 3
BINAH

Title: Understanding

Description: Ama—the dark sterile mother, Aima—the bright fertile mother, Mara—the great sea, Khorsia—the throne, form, vessel of dynamic force, womb of all life, perceptive awareness, intuition

Associated Keywords: Limitation, form, constraint, fertility, infertility, incarnation, karma, time, natural law, containment, the womb and gestation

Spiritual Experience: Vision of sorrow

Path: Third Path of Wisdom, the Sanctifying Intelligence, the Foundation of Primordial Wisdom, the creation of Faith

Virtue: Silence

Vice: Avarice

God Name: Jehovah Elohim

Archangel: Tzaphkiel, contemplation of God, the prince of the spiritual strife against evil

Angelic Order: Aralim, the Mighty One, Thrones

Image: Matron

Planet: Shabbathai, Saturn

Element: Root of Water

Colors:

    Atziluth—crimson

    Briah—black

    Yetzirah—dark brown

    Assiah—grey flecked with pink

Physical Body: Right side of the face

Symbols: Cup, female sex organs

Plant: Cypress, poppy

Animal: Woman

Incense: Myrrh, civet

Metal: Lead

Stone: Sapphire

Human Focus: None

Correspondences in Other Pantheons:

    Egyptian—Mat

    Greek—Rhea

    Roman—Magna Mater

    Scandinavian—Frigga

    Hindu—Saraswati, Kali

SEPHIRA 0
DAATH

Although this sephira has no number, it sits between Chokmah and Binah and must follow next.

Title: Knowledge

Description: The Unmanifested, realization, illumination, knowledge gained through experience of life on all levels; it is also knowledge in the biblical sense, as Adam "knowing" Eve, and thus it is sex or union on a higher spiritual level

This is not a true Sephira and therefore has no correspondences.

SEPHIRA 4
CHESED

Title: Mercy

Description: Compassion, greatness, grace, majesty, higher love, protecting father, receptivity, beneficence

Associated Keywords: Gedulah, authority, inspiration, vision, leadership, service

Spiritual Experience: Vision of love

Path: Fourth Path of Wisdom, the Arresting or Receiving Intelligence

Virtue: Obedience

Vice: Tyranny

God Name: El

Archangel: Tzadkiel, justice of God, prince of mercy

Angelic Order: Hashmalim, Brilliant Ones, Dominions

Image: Crowned and throned king

Planet: Tzadekh, Jupiter

Element: Water

Colors:

Atziluth—deep violet

Briah—blue

Yetzirah—purple

Assiah—azure, flecked with yellow

Physical Body: Left arm

Symbols: Orb, tetrahedron

Plant: Olive, shamrock

Animal: Unicorn

Incense: Cedar

Metal: Tin

Stone: Amethyst

Human Focus: Journeys, banks, debts, gambling, abundance, prosperity, growth

Correspondences in Other Pantheons:

Egyptian—Ptah

Greek—Zeus

Roman—Jupiter

Scandinavian—Balder

Hindu—Rama Chandra

SEPHIRAH 5
GEBURAH

Title: Severity, Strength

Description: Control of power by discipline and duty, justice, severity, judgment

Associated Keywords: Pachad—fear; Din—justice, power, retribution, cruelty, oppression, domination, severity, martial arts

Spiritual Experience: Vision of power

Path: Fifth Path of Wisdom, the Radical Intelligence

Virtue: Courage

Vice: Destruction

God Name: Elohim Gebor

Archangel: Kamael, severity of God

Angelic Order: Seraphim, Flaming Serpents, Powers

Image: Warrior in his chariot

Planet: Madim, Mars

Element: Fire

Colors:

    Atziluth—orange

    Briah—red

    Yetzirah—scarlet

    Assiah—red, flecked with black

Physical Body: Right arm

Symbols: Pentagon, sword

Plant: Oak

Animal: Basilisk

Incense: Tobacco

Metal: Iron

Stone: Ruby

Human Focus: Dangers, wars, surgery, construction, destruction, enemies

Correspondences in Other Pantheons:

    Egyptian—Seth

    Greek—Ares

    Roman—Mars

Scandinavian—Loki

Hindu—Shiva

SEPHIRA 6
TIPHARETH

Title: Beauty

Description: Universal health, harmony, happiness in life, equilibrium, balance, clemency

Associated Keywords: Zoar Anpin—the Lesser Countenance, Melekh—the King, Adam—the Son, the Man, the Self, the Son of God, the Philosophers' Stone, identity, the Great Work

Spiritual Experience: Vision of harmony

Path: Sixth Path of Wisdom, the Intelligence of the Mediating Influence

Virtue: Devotion to the Great Work

Vice: Pride

God Name: Jehovah elo ve Daath

Archangel: Raphael, divine physician

Angelic Order: Malachim, Kings, Virtues

Image: Majestic king, a child, a sacrificed king

Planet: Shemesh, the Sun

Element: Air

Colors:

Atziluth—rose pink

Briah—yellow

Yetzirah—salmon pink

Assiah—amber

Physical Body: Breast

Symbol: Cube

Plant: Acacia, vine, bay, laurel

Animal: Lion

Incense: Olibanum

Metal: Gold

Stone: Topaz

Human Focus: Success, money, power, superiors, mental powers, health

Correspondences in Other Pantheons:

Egyptian—Ra

Greek—Apollo

Roman—Helios

Scandinavian—Thor

Hindu—Indra / Surya

SEPHIRA 7
NETZACH

Title: Victory

Description: Achievement, firmness, instincts, emotions, illusions, physical love

Associated Keywords: Passion, pleasure, luxury, sensual beauty, feelings, love, hate, anger, joy, depression, misery, excitement, desire, lust, empathy, sympathy

Spiritual Experience: Vision of Beauty Triumphant

Path: Seventh Path of Wisdom, the Hidden Intelligence

Virtue: Unselfishness

Vice: Lust

God Name: Jehovah Tzabaoth

Archangel: Haniel, Grace of God

Angelic Order: Elohim, Gods, Principalities

Image: Lovely naked woman

Planet: Nogah, Venus

Element: Fire

Colors:

    Atziluth—amber

    Briah—emerald green

    Yetzirah—yellow green

    Assiah—olive, flecked with gold

Physical Body: Left loin, hip, leg

Symbols: Rose, lamp, and girdle

Plant: Rose

Animal: Lynx

Incense: Benzoin

Metal: Copper

Stone: Emerald

Human Focus: Love, passion, marriage, women, arts, music, enjoyment, pleasure, friends

Correspondences in Other Pantheons:

    Egyptian—Hathor

    Greek—Aphrodite

    Roman—Venus

    Scandinavian—Freya

    Hindu—Sita

SEPHIRA 8
HOD

Title: Glory

Description: The Perfect and Absolute Intelligence, reason, abstraction, communication

Associated Keywords: Ritual magic, language, speech, science

Spiritual Experience: Vision of Splendor

Path: Eighth Path of Wisdom, the depths of the Sphere of Magnificence

Virtue: Truthfulness

Vice: Dishonesty

God Name: Elohim Tzabaoth

Archangel: Michael, he who is like God

Angelic Order: Beni Elohim, Sons of God, Archangels

Image: Hermaphrodite

Planet: Mercury

Element: Water

Colors:

Atziluth—violet

Briah—orange

Yetzirah—brick red

Assiah—yellowish black, flecked with white

Physical Body: Right loin, hip, leg

Symbols: Names, versicles, apron

Plant: Moly

Animal: Hermaphrodite

Incense: Storax

Metal: Quicksilver

Stone: Opal

Human Focus: Papers, business matters, books, contracts

Correspondences in Other Pantheons:

Egyptian—Anubis

Greek—Hermes

Roman—Mercury

Scandinavian—Freya

Hindu—Hanuman

SEPHIRA 9
YESOD

Title: Foundation

Description: The Purified Intelligence, sphere of astral light, sphere of the Moon, receptacle of emanations of other Sephiroth

Associated Keywords: Perception, imagination, glamour, the Unconscious, tides, dreams, divination, astral plane, sex and reproduction, psychism

Spiritual Experience: Vision of the Machinery of the Universe

Path: Ninth Path of Wisdom, establishes unity among the Sephiroth

Virtue: Independence

Vice: Idleness

God Name: Adonai Ha Aretz

Archangel: Gabriel, Man-God

Angelic Order: Cherubim, Angels

Image: Beautiful naked man

Planet: Levanah, the Moon

Element: Air

Colors:

Atziluth—indigo

Briah—violet

Yetzirah—dark purple

Assiah—citrine, flecked with azure

Physical Body: Reproductive organs

Symbols: Perfumes, sandals

Plant: Mandrake, damiana

Animal: Elephant

Incense: Jasmine

Metal: Silver

Stone: White quartz

Human Focus: Affairs of women, the mother, changes, moves, short trips

Correspondences in Other Pantheons:

Egyptian—Isis

Greek—Artemis

Roman—Diana

Scandinavian—Sif

Hindu—Lakshmi

SEPHIRA IO
MALKUTH

Title: The Kingdom

Description: The Resplendent Intelligence, material world, sphere of nature, sphere of the Shekinah, Malkah—the Queen, Inferior Mother, Gate of Death, Gate of Eden, Gate of Justice, Kallah—the Bride, the Virgin

Associated Keywords: Mother Earth, physical elements, natural world, possessions, inertia, physical death, incarnation, the four elements

Spiritual Experience: Vision of the Holy Guardian Angel

Path: Tenth Path of Wisdom, has its seat in Binah

Virtue: Discrimination, discernment

Vice: Inertia

God Name: Shaddai El Chai

Archangel: Sandalphon, twin brother of Metraton

Angelic Order: Ishim, the blessed souls of the just

Image: Young woman, crowned and throned

Planet: Cholem Yesodeth, the Earth

Element: Earth

Colors:

Atziluth—Yellow

Briah—citrine, olive, russet, black

Yetzirah—citrine, olive, russet, black, flecked with yellow

Assiah—black, rayed with yellow

Physical Body: feet, anus

Symbol: Equal-armed cross

Plant: Lily, ivy

Animal: Sphinx

Incense: Dittany of Crete

Metal: Rock, mica

Stone: Rock crystal

Human Focus: Energy, matter and material things

Correspondences in Other Pantheons:

Egyptian—Nephthys

Greek—Demeter

Roman—Ceres

Scandinavian—Nerthus

Hindu—Ganesh

BIBLIOGRAPHY

Agrippa, C., *De Occulta Philosophia*, New York, 1971.

Allen, A. C., *The Skin: A Clinicopathological Treatise*, New York, 1967.

Anderson, P., *Science in Defense of Liberal Religion*, London, 1933.

Appian of Alexandria, *Romaica (History of Rome)*, New York, 1960.

Apocrypha, New York, 1987.

Aristotle, *Metaphysics*, trans. Hope, R., New York, 1988.

Bardon, F., *The Key to the True Quabbalah*, Austria, 1971.

Beagon, M., *Roman Nature: The Thought of Pliny the Elder*, New York, 1992.

Bible, St. James Version, New York, 1984.

Bible, New Revised Standard Version (Harper Collins Study Bible), New York, 1989.

Cambridge History of India, London, 1968.

Charlesworth, J. H., "Jesus and Jehohanan: An Archeological Note on Crucifixion," *Expository Times*, Edinburgh, 1973.

———, ed., *The Old Testament Pseudoepigrapha: Second Book of Enoch*, New York, 1980.

———, and Kiley, M., *The Lord's Prayer and Other Prayer Texts from the Greco-Roman Era*, Philadelphia, 1994.

Churchland, P. M., *Matter and Consciousness*, Cambridge, Mass., 1988.

Cicero, *The Republic and Its Laws*, trans. Grant, M., New York, 1980.

———, *Selected Works*, trans. Grant, M., New York, 1960.

Crossan, J. D., *Jesus, A Revolutionary Biography*, New York, 1994.

Darwin, C., *The Origin of Species*, New York, 1993.

Davies, P., *God and the New Physics*, London, 1983.

———, *The Mind of God*, Adelaide, 1996.

Edwards, W. D., et al., "On the Physical Death of Jesus Christ," *Journal of the American Medical Association*, March, 1986.

Einstein, *Ideas and Opinions*, New York, 1992.

———, *Relativity, The Special and General Theory*, New York, 1995.

Fishman, Dr. Gerald J., The Burst and Transient Source Experiment, NASA (ongoing).

Fortune, D., *The Mystical Qabalah*, London, 1935.

Franck, A., *The Kabbalah*, London, 1926.

Gaer, J., *How the Great Religions Began*, London, 1954.

Gamow, G., *The Creation of the Universe*, New York, 1974.

———, *Thirty Years that Shook Physics: The Story of Quantum Theory*, New York, 1985.

Gaster, T. H., *The Dead Sea Scriptures*, New York, 1964.

Ginsburg, C. D., *The Kabbalah*, London, 1863.

Gleick, P., *Chaos*, New York, 1987.

González-Wippler, M., *A Kabbalah for the Modern World*, St. Paul, 1998.

Guthrie, K. S., *The Pythagorean Sourcebook and Library*, New Jersey, 1991.

Hahn, E., and Benes, B. L., *Breath of God*, New York, 1985.

Herodotus, *The Histories*, trans. A. de Selincourt, New York, 1996.

Hawking, S., *A Brief History of Time*, New York, 1988.

———, *The Universe in a Nutshell*, New York, 2001.

Jastrow, R., *God and the Astronomers*, New York, 1977.

Josephus, F., *The Works of Josephus: Complete and Unabridged*, New York, 1980.

Jung, C. G., *The Archetypes of the Collective Unconscious*, Volume 9, Part 1, New Jersey, 1981.

———, *The Structure and Dynamics of the Psyche*, New York, 1960.

———, *Mysterium Coniunctionis*, New York, 1963.

Kant, I., *Prolegomena to Any Future Metaphysics*, New York, 1951.

Kaplan, A., transl., *Sepher Yetzirah*, Boston, 1997.

Klein, E., *Kabbalah of Creation*, New Jersey, 2000.

Knight, G., *A Practical Guide to Kabbalistic Symbolism*, London, 1965.

Krakovsky, L. I., *Kabbalah, the Light of Redemption*, Israel, 1970.

Lederman, L., *The God Particle*, New York, 1993.

Levy, F., *Pauli Sententiae: A Palingenesia of the Opening Titles as a Specimen of Research on West Roman Vulgar Law*, New York, 1970.

Luria, I., *Ten Luminous Emanations*, Israel, 1969.

———, *Kabbalah of Creation*, trans. E. Klein, New Jersey, 2000.

Luzzatto, M. C., *General Principles of the Kabbalah*, New York, 1970.

Maimonides, M., *A Guide to the Perplexed*, New York, 1956.

———, *Mishneh Torah*, New York, 1974.

Mason, S., *Josephus and the New Testament*, New York, 1995.

Mathers, S. L. M., *The Kabbalah Unveiled*, New York, 1971.

Meier, J. P., *A Marginal Jew: Rethinking the Historical Jesus*, New York, 1991.

Myer, I., *Qabbalah*, New York, 1970.

Nietszche, F., *Thus Spake Zarathustra*, New York, 1999.

Potter, C. F., *The Lost Years of Jesus Revealed*, Connecticut, 1962.

Seneca, *Letters from a Stoic: Epistulae Morales Ad Lucilium*, New York, 1969.

Ouspensky, P., *Tertium Organum: A Key to the Enigmas of the Universe*, New York, 1968.

Pfeiffer, C. F., *The Dead Sea Scrolls and the Bible*, New York, 1972.

Platt, R. H., *The Forgotten Books of Eden*, New York, 1980.

Popper, K. and Eccles, J. C., *The Self and Its Brain*, Berlin, 1977.

Progoff, I., *Jung, Synchronicity and Human Destiny*, New York, 1973.

Regardie, *A Garden of Pomegranates*, St. Paul, 1970.

————, *The Golden Dawn*, St. Paul, 1986.

Robinson, I., *Moses Cordovero's Introduction to Kabbalah*, New York, 1994.

St. Augustine, *Confessions of St. Augustine*, London, 1982.

————, *The City of God*, New York, 1972.

St. Iranaeus of Lyons, *Against the Heresies*, trans. Unger, D. J., New York, 1985.

St. Thomas Aquinas, *Summa Theologica*, New York, 1997.

Schoeps, H. J., *The Jewish-Christian Argument*, New York, 1963.

Scholem, G., *Major Trends in Jewish Mysticism*, New York, 1954.

————, *On the Kabbalah and Its Symbolism*, New York, 1965.

Seneca, *Letters from a Stoic: Epistulae Morales Ad Lucilium*, New York, 1969.

Suares, C., ed., *The Sepher Yetzirah, the Book of Formation*, London, 1968.

————, *The Cipher of Genesis*, Berkeley, 1970.

Talmadge, F. E., *Disputation and Dialogue: Readings in the Jewish-Christian Encounter*, New York, 1975.

Tipler, F. J., *The Physics of Immortality*, New York, 1994.

Torah Anthology (The Me'am Lo'ez), trans. Kaplan, A., New York, 1988.

Trachtenberg, J., *Jewish Magic and Mysticism*, New York, 1961.

Waite, A. E., *The Holy Kabbalah*, New York, 1960.

Weiner, H., *Nine and a Half Mystics: The Kabbalah Today*, New York, 1969.

Westcott, W. W., ed., *The Sepher Yetzirah, the Book of Formation*, London, 1967.

Whiston, W., trans., *The Works of Flavius Josephus*, New York, 1988.

Yonge, C. D., ed., *The Works of Philo: Complete and Unabridged*, New York, 1993.

Zohar, the Book of Splendor, G. Scholem, ed., New York, 1949.

Zugibe, F., *Cross and the Shroud: A Medical Enquiry into the Crucifixion*, New York, 1982.

INDEX

THE ULTIMATE KEY

Do not unseal these pages now. Read the entire book and wait a week before unsealing the pages. During this week, study Jesus's commandments as they apply to the ten Sephiroth of the Tree of Life. You should also re-read chapter 7, Letters of Light, especially the part that discusses the binary system. At the end of the week, unseal the insert by slitting the perforated pages to get the Secret Message and the Ultimate Key.

open at perforation

$\longrightarrow$